In the Arms
of the Angels

T0358158

For Billy

This is a true story, however, some names of the persons referred to within the text of this book have been changed in order to protect their privacy. Although the author and publisher have exhaustively researched to ensure the accuracy of the information contained in this book, we assume no responsibility for errors, inaccuracies, omissions or any other inconsistency herein. Any slight against people or organizations is unintentional.

In the Arms
of the Angels

Kim A. Patra

**Wakefield
Press**

Wakefield Press
1 The Parade West
Kent Town
South Australia 5067
www.wakefieldpress.com.au

First published 2003 by Saritaksu Design Communication, Bali
Wakefield Press edition published 2004
Copyright © Kim A. Patra, 2003, 2004

Design by Saritaksu Design Communication, Bali
Photos courtesy of Dr. Art Sorrell, U.C.L.A Medical Center
"Hands" by Anak Agung Cahyadi
Printed and bound by Hyde Park Press, Adelaide

National Library of Australia
Cataloguing-in-publication entry

Patra, Kim A.
In the arms of the angels.

ISBN 1 86254 643 6.

1. Patra, Kim A. 2. Bali Bombings, Kuta, Bali, Indonesia, 2002 –
Personal narratives. 3. Terrorism – Indonesia – Bali Island.
4. Mass casualties – Indonesia – Bali Island. I. Title.

303.625095986

Wakefield Press thanks Fox Creek Wines
and Arts South Australia for their support.

Contents

Acknowledgements

I would like to express my appreciation to the following people for being a part of my life, a part of this book and a part of the all that it means to so many people:

Mum and Dad for all their financial support and for letting me go to do the things that I had to do.

My children Indah, Ben, & Krisna for accepting my absence.

Putu 'T' for just 'being there'.

Mark Keatinge, Katrina Maja, Anne & Paul Christie, and Melina Caruso for all their support and proof reading.

Dr. David & Claire Marsh for helping me to recall the events in this book.

Natalie for sharing her bitter memories.

Dr. Eric Savitsky and his team at the U.C.L.A. Center for Emergency and Trauma Medicine, for sharing their knowledge.

Charles "Chuck" Christian E.M.T. (Emergency Medicine Technician) for all his teachings.

Anak Agung Cahyadi ('Cah') for his art and his music.

Sandra McArthur for giving me the courage to be me.

Foreword

When the world thinks of Bali now, they don't just think of exotic Hindu temples, sun washed beaches and world class resorts. Bali is now sadly remembered for one of the most devastating terrorist bomb attacks that the world has known.

Most residents of southern Bali had heard the blast, and soon found out the basic details of what had transpired, trying to make some attempt to digest the immensity of what this meant. The local grapevine worked overtime through the tropical predawn and as the sun rose, an amazing voluntary effort began to unfold at the local general hospital.

Thankfully for us all, teams of medical volunteers, one of whom was Kim Patra, were already there. As they worked alongside the Australian Consular officials, they were able to directly assist the victims as well as give us guidance on how best we would be able to help.

Kim is an Australian registered nurse and midwife and a long time resident of Bali. Many long term expatriates here have benefited by her calm and considerate expertise at some time or another, ranging from telephone advice for minor ailments to being accompanied by her on medical evacuations overseas.

'In the Arms of the Angels' is a very honest and personal account by Kim as she relives the first traumatic days at Sanglah General Hospital. It recounts a story that only she could tell.

The respect that Kim has from us here in Bali and her ability to lovingly 'tell it as it is', combined with her dedicated professionalism meant that she played a pivotal role in the incredible team effort to minimize the death toll and complications arising from the injuries in the first hours and days after that attack.

Kim, with the help of another local expatriate nurse, Chrissie

O'Connor, was able to almost immediately set up a workable interface in the hospitals between the overwhelmed local medical professionals, the foreign volunteer doctors and nurses and an army of inexperienced volunteers that were 'ready to help, just tell me how!'.

There is no city in the world that could have dealt with such an event in a faultlessly prepared manner. Even after having a full day to prepare, many of the major Australian hospitals were still stretched to the limit and could only each accept a small proportion of the evacuated injured.

There were so many things that will never be forgotten here. Some are:

- The incredible effort by the entire Sanglah General Hospital staff in Bali. Against overwhelming odds, and with little experience in mass casualty trauma, their readiness to accept and to direct all the assistance that was offered saved the lives of so many.
- The miraculous appearance of those medical professionals on vacation, all of them with pertinent specialist expertise, who alongside the local staff were performing critical emergency operations in the wards to save life and limb.
- The extraordinary outpouring of volunteers from the local community, helping in wards, handling enquiries, and most sadly, working to assist in identifying the dead.
- The timely arrival of the evacuation team from Australia, all organized and on the ground in less than 24 hours.

For many of us here in Bali the most vivid memories of all are those of incredible sadness as we worked amongst the dead at the hospital morgue witnessing the pain of their grieving families and friends as well as the bravery of those so terribly hurt, enduring unimaginable injuries without complaint and often with great humor.

Kim's story is our story, the story of the witnesses to all that happened in the first days after the bomb.

We can only pray that this story never needs to be told again.

Mark Keatinge
Bali, August 2003

Introduction

Having lived on the island of Bali for the best part of twenty years, I have become a veteran of the island lifestyle and have a sound knowledge of the Balinese culture and religion. Born in the South West of England, and raised in Adelaide, South Australia, I was probably the least likely of people that one would have expected to make her home on the sleepy island of Bali. Married at an early age, and an ambitious professional, I was prompted by the woes of divorce and the increasing pressures of working in the public health care system to seek a two week refuge on a tropical island. Little did I know that this experience would seduce me into several more long visits before my daughter (then five years of age) and I eventually made it our home.

Windsurfing and romance were the lures that caught me, and along with an enterprising water sports operation in Sanur I started one of the first windsurfing schools on the island. After less than a year of sun, wind and surf, marriage, pregnancy and the usual financial pressures it became clear that the income from the windsurfing club would no longer pay the bills (although the cost of living was considerably cheaper then). A small garments business that at its best consisted of three retail stores on the main Sanur strip became our main source of income for the next fifteen years. The single remaining outlet of 'Naga Naga Design' finally closed its doors in November of 2001, only two months after the tragedy of 9/11 had sent tourism plummeting to levels that could no longer make the business a viable operation.

My marriage to a Balinese and a native of Sanur lasted seven very long years, before the effects of night-clubbing, numerous affairs, gambling and an interfering mother-in-law finally took its toll. I filed for divorce in 1994 and became a naturalized Indonesian Citizen in order to be able to stay on the island and retain custody of my children (highly unusual in Bali as it is a strictly patriarchal society). Following divorce and several short-lived relationships that could only be termed as mishaps, I became involved with a friend and fellow musician Gede Tony. We have remained close companions ever since.

Throughout these years I had become increasingly involved with health care, that started with tending cuts, boils, ear infections and other ills that plagued the surfers, tourists and family members of the local Sanur community.

After birthing my second son in a Denpasar hospital it became blatantly obvious that the local obstetric services were less than what most western women would expect. My scant 'barefoot doctor' practice expanded to an antenatal and postnatal care program that would support other (mostly expatriate) women throughout their pregnancies on the island.

During a chance introduction to a medical scout from Jakarta in 1993 I was interviewed and signed on as a flying nurse escort. Since then over sixty medical evacuation cases have taken me to all four corners of the globe assisting tourists and expatriates, stricken with all nature of injury or disease. Through various other connections in the local health sector, I was introduced to a group of international businessmen and was instrumental in the initial phase of one of the more highly respected tourist clinics on the island. Since my term at the clinic ended I have resumed my interest in women's and children's health, and after seven long years of processing have finally been accepted into the Association of Indonesian Midwives (I.B.I.). I now run my own private practice from my Sanur residence.

Over the span of these two decades Bali has undergone significant changes. When I first settled on the island in the mid 1980's we had to drive ten kilometers to the island's capital in order to purchase even a battery or a light globe, the strongest of which you could usually find was 25 watts! Telephones were few and far between, and private home phones were (for obvious reasons) well guarded and locked. Delicacies such as chocolate, cheese and wine were just not available. This is a stark comparison to the internet cafe culture of today and the array of delights that one can find at the many gourmet delicatessens that are now scattered throughout the island.

In the early days communicating with my family in Australia was an exercise in itself having to pay ridiculous prices at the local 'WARTEL' (communication post) for an international connection, or rely on the local mail service. A letter to Australia would usually take two to three weeks if it was ever delivered at all! It makes me wonder how we ever coped, when with today's technology I can send a message directly to my daughter's cell phone in Australia in less time that it takes to seal an envelope or paste a postage stamp! Internet technology now brings world news to our homes and offices in an instant, and gone are the days of our insular existence when local newspapers and television (if you had one) brought only snippets of censored international affairs, and an outdated Sydney Herald was breaking news.

Bali has since progressed in leaps and bounds with several significant events heralding major changes. The currency crash of 1997 brought international investors clamoring for property bargains; the fall of the Soeharto government saw the exodus of the ethnic Chinese community from the troubled capital of Jakarta to the shores of the 'peaceful' island, and Bali's metropolitan population seemed to double almost overnight. Some changes would be for the better but some would be catastrophic. Hectares of mangrove swamp would be transformed into mega shopping malls or cleared for state of the art water sports facilities that would not get any further than the blueprints. Ancient religious sites were desecrated and earmarked for 'Disneyland-like' attractions that would never be completed. Traditional bamboo food stalls (warungs) would be replaced by 24/7 stores whose garish red and white neon signs flashed out across the main roads and freeways.

Progress saw the upgrading of the international airport from a stifling tin and hardboard shed to a sprawling multi storey ultra-modern facility housing duty free shops, V.V.I.P. executive lounges, and real bathrooms!

The basic one-roomed cold shower with fan and breakfast 'losmens' (local inns) were being replaced by the ever popular and luxurious Villa style accommodation; the standard one hour coconut oil rub on the beach had been upgraded to aroma-therapeutic massage at some of the most opulent spa houses in the world. The international franchise giants had also come to town and brands such as McDonalds, Kentucky Fried Chicken, Wendys, Dunkin Donuts, Hagaan Daaz, and Planet Hollywood had became household names. The infamous 'Wayans Warung' that had once sold the best fried rice and fresh juice on the Island, (but the worst hamburgers!) had been replaced by a monument to modern architecture, The Hard Rock Café.

While there was no doubt that Bali had certainly seen some major changes both for the better and for the worse, nothing would affect the island as much as the senseless and horrific assault that she suffered on the night of October the 12th, 2002. Two massive explosions ripped through two of the most popular night clubs on the island, the Sari Club, and Paddy's Bar, killing most of the Saturday night revelers and engulfing passers-by as they strolled along the busy Kuta street. The world would mourn the deaths of over two hundred people from twenty one nations. Australia would suffer the largest ever loss of life in peace time, losing eightyeight citizens. Hundreds more were injured and maimed, both physically and emotionally scarred. Families had been ripped apart with some not losing one but two or three family members. Sporting clubs, rugby and football teams suffered massive losses, including the Western Australian Kingsley Park team that lost seven of its players.

In the days, weeks and months that followed a mammoth team of volunteers and professionals from every walk of life would tackle the nightmare that was to follow the 'Bali Bomb'. Ordinary people would perform extraordinary tasks. They would give more in time, talent, and monetary support than could ever have been thought possible.

This book has been written from the view point of a medical volunteer (myself) and may differ from others who have an alternate stand-point or over-view of the situation. Many of the names have been changed in order to protect the privacy of those concerned, and in respect for the deceased. The events recollected in this book are true. This is my story, a dedication to all the workers, the individuals, the teams and organizations that contributed to the massive task that was performed.

From youths who toiled through the smoke and the heat to retrieve the dead and rescue the wounded, to the young man that went 'back for his mates' and was never seen again.

From the barman that poured cold beer on to the scorched flesh of a burned man, to the team of youths that repeatedly rammed a vehicle into a fire hydrant until its water ran freely.

From the boys and men who ferried victims to the hospital on motor bikes, cars and trucks, to the teams of flying 'angels' that manned the Hercules aircraft.

From the junior nurse who held the hand of a dying man, to the teams of surgeons and doctors that would piece together those that could be saved.

From the men, women and children that kept bedside vigil for the wounded and dying, to the hotels, restaurants and other corporations that donated all manner of goods.

From the language teacher that gave her skills for the young wounded French girl, to the teams of consular staff that would work day in and day out without reprise.

From the men and women who cared for the dead or what remained of them, to the ice and wood companies that provided as much as they could to preserve their remains.

From the school girl who gave up her pocket money for the victims, to those that formed organizations that would govern and support the cause.

Without pride or prejudice, this book is for them.

1
Signs

Saturday, October the 12th

Saturday night and we all settled in front of the television to watch tonight's chosen movie 'Signs'. I was determined to get to see the entire movie this time with no interruptions. My boys, Ben (13), and Krisna (10), had been complaining that I never spent enough time with them, so Saturday evenings had been designated as movie night, and I was bound to watch whatever they had chosen. Tonight's choice wasn't that bad, even though the DVD was a copy, the quality was acceptable.

The creepy alien fingers that slid around Mel Gibson's door had us all on the edge of our seats. How could we have known of the true horror that was imminent and just minutes away? Once the aliens were defeated it was time for bed.

"I want milk and cookies, I want milk and cookies!" Kris demanded. After obliging his request and with the bed-time ritual fulfilled, both Ben and Kris were ready for slumber.

I took the dishes downstairs as Tony, my longterm companion, turned off the television. Unlike other Balinese who often adopted a western name for ease of the western tongue, 'Tony' was his real name ('Gede Tony' to be precise). All but one of his five brothers had been given western names by their enterprising father, who was once one of the most successful businessmen on the island back in the boom of the 60's & 70's. Tony's parents were both ordained Hindu priests now which was fine by me. I had already had quite enough of interfering in-laws with my former Balinese husband and father of my sons. As priests, Tony's parents could not concern themselves with the earthly affairs of their children, or anything else for that matter. They were now vessels of the Gods and the spirit world.

Tony and I would never marry. After two failed marriages and three children, I had given up on the nuptials. Both of my previous marriages had lasted seven years, Tony and I had now been together for just as long and I felt no desire to consecrate the relationship. He was my best friend and we shared everything; our lives, our feelings, our music; pain, pleasure and bad gas, there were no secrets.

I prepared to lock up the house for the night; I lifted the heavy ironwood bar that locked the huge carved wooden doors and as I slide the bar into its cradle the doors seemed to thrust against me. "It must be one of the dogs that I had forgotten to let in." I thought, but the dogs were both inside.

"Wah! . . . did you feel that?" Tony said.

"Mum the curtains all blew in, what was it?"

"Oh it's nothing, probably just the wind," I replied (on a completely still October night!).

It was something, I knew it was something, but the boys need not concern themselves with it. They were tired and sleep came quickly.

"What do you think it was Kim?" Tony was as puzzled as I was. "You should have seen the curtains, they blew in from all sides . . . it wasn't the wind."

We looked out of the upstairs window for some sign of the phenomenon that had rocked our Sanur house. The skies were clear and still. No sign of thunder, nothing very unusual at all. Across the paddies we had an uninterrupted view of the volcanoes that lined the horizon.

"A volcano perhaps?" I thought out loud for some explanation; but the mountains stood silent and black against the night sky.

I half expected my phone to ring, but it was Tony's phone that rang first. I could hear his brother's voice on the end of the line and he seemed to be shouting. Four of the six brothers were professional musicians including Tony. Tony's older brother was playing in Kuta tonight.

"Where are you?" Tony's brother's voice sounded distressed.

"At home with Kim watching movies, what's up?"

"Stay there. Don't come out. Something's happened in Kuta. I think the petrol station has gone up. There's fire everywhere. Where are the other brothers? Where are they playing?"

"Don't know . . . in Ubud I think?"

There was another call, another garbled message,

"Someone says something about a bomb." Tony said with a puzzled look.

"A bomb? In Bali? No way!"

The musicians' grapevine was running hot. Two more calls from musicians confirmed that something terrible had happened. No one knew exactly what, but the location was given as Legian street, near Paddys Pub. We discussed it briefly and decided that it was probably an explosion of bottled gas in a restaurant (all cooking here is done with LPG gas, and the commercial kitchen tanks are huge).

My thoughts reeled as I remembered a conversation that I had heard at the International School on the previous day. I had been employed by the Bali International School (B.I.S.) as the school nurse just a few months ago, so I knew most of the students there. Many of the high school students were going to Paddys to farewell the graduates that were going overseas to study.

"Oh my God Tony! Elena's boys will be there!"

Elena had been a dear friend for many years. Her boys had once gone to school with Ben and Kris, and our families had since remained close.

I dialed her number. It was midnight but she answered the phone almost immediately. "Elena, listen where are the boys, Mikio, Teo, where are they?"

"It's okay, it's okay, they're on there way back to Sanur. What's happened anyway?"

Elena never seemed to get upset about anything, and her Swiss-Italian accent expressed only curious concern. She would later learn that both Mikio and Teo, along with almost every other expatriate senior high student on the island had come minutes if not seconds away from losing their lives.

I toyed with the idea of going, but going to where I did not know. If it really was a gas explosion or a petrol station fire, I was not going anywhere near it. I could hear the thick Denver voice of our paramedic lecturer, Chuck, as clear as if it were yesterday.

"Does anyone in the class know how close you can get to a gas tanker to assist any victims that may be injured?" He spoke like a trooper and had been trained as such. "No? Well the answer is you don't go! You get the hell away from that baby, in fact you get so far away that when you look back if that tanker looks any bigger than you're thumb nail you're too damn close!"

With Chuck's words still ringing in my ears, I settled down for the night. No-one had called, I mustn't be needed. Tony went home to a family pow-wow with all five brothers who had safely returned home.

Sunday, October 13th, 05.30 am

The phone rang, and as modern technology would have it, I knew it was David Chaplin the Australian Vice-Consul, before I even took the call. I thought he must have problems with his baby daughter, a cold or flu perhaps, breast-feeding problems maybe? The previous nights events had temporarily eluded me in my wakening stupor.

"Morning David, what's up?"

"Hi Kim, sorry to call you so early. Would you mind coming to give us a bit of a hand in Sanglah?"

David was the kind of person that would have sounded cheerful looking directly into the arms of Armageddon. He was a tall and lanky chap, always a smile, the 'boy-next-door' type, whom I would not have credited with the intestinal fortitude to handle a tyre blow-out let alone a full on disaster, but on this day however my character judgment was to be proven very, very wrong.

"Sure, David what's going on?"

"We're not sure at this stage, I can't say too much except that a lot of Australians have been hurt, looks like it was intentional. Actually it's a mess in here . . . it's a bloody mess mate!"

"I'll be there in about forty-five minutes."

"Good, I'll meet you at the emergency room entrance. Give me a call when you're on your way."

I had a quick shower and dressed for comfort and speed, in T-shirt, pants, and a very old, very well worn pair of sneakers. I grabbed my medi-vac pack from the cupboard thinking it might be of some use, although it was equipped to take one or at most two patients on aero-medical evacuations, not to treat hundreds! I had better take my old white nurse's jacket I thought. This along with a stethoscope slung around my neck would get me through doors not normally open to the public at Sanglah hospital.

My thoughts reeled as I checked for everything that I would need to do before I left for the hospital. The kids! What to do with the kids?! I'd write them a quick note and the maid would be here at eight. She'd get breakfast and sort things out then. I scrawled them a quick message and left it on the sink. Kris always cleaned his teeth first thing - he'd find the note then.

I'd better write a note to Mum as well. She would be bound to hear something on the news and panic. "MUM & DAD," I wrote in sprawling black letters "SOME ? TERRORIST ATTACKS IN BALI.

BOMBS HAVE EXPLODED IN SEVERAL NIGHT CLUBS, RES-
TAURANTS. WE ARE OK. WILL KEEP YOU POSTED . . . KIM."
I fed it through the fax machine hoping that Dad would find it before
they watched the morning news in Adelaide.

I piled a few bits and pieces into a waist-bag, I would need both
hands free, and would not have time to concern myself with hand-
bags. I would need some loose change, my phone, tissues and a pen.
There would be a clipboard in my pack, but I'd better take some
extra paper and my passport just in case.

Breakfast would be wise and I could eat a banana and a muesli
bar in the car on the way. The dogs looked on curiously as I loaded
up the car. They were used to seeing me leave at a minute's notice
and the big red back-pack meant I would be gone for not much more
than a day, if I took a suitcase it meant I would be away longer. I
piled my pack into the old Peugeot and fired up the engine. She
started! That was a bonus! I coaxed her along as we reversed out of
the driveway. "That's it old girl, don't give-out on me today, we've
got too much to do."

The 1984 dark green Peugeot sedan was the most comfortable
car I had ever driven. Lately though, it seemed that her disease was
terminal. She was leaking over a liter of oil a week and even Tony
could not fix it. (Tony could fix ANYTHING, or at least Kris thought
so!) Financially times were already hard, so for the time being at
least she was my only steed.

The car was hardly out of the drive when the phone rang. It was
Kris, he was a very light sleeper and he had heard me leave.
"Mummy . . . where are you going?"

"I have to go my love. Remember the noise we heard last night?
Some people have been hurt. Mummy's got to help them, you know
how it is."

"Are you going to Singapore? Will we get presents?" I always brought presents when I came back from a case. It was a kind of 'pay off' for having to leave them for a day or two.

"No presents today my love. I'll be in Denpasar."

"Aww . . . who's going to take me to soccer?" There was a muffled voice in the background, ". . . . and Ben wants to know what's for breakfast?"

"There'll be no soccer today my love. You can have whatever's in the fridge for breakfast. Ketut (the maid) will be there soon. Tell Ben he mustn't go far, better for you both to stay home today."

"But why?"

"Just do as I say, Mummy's got to go now. I'll call you guys later. I don't know what time I'll be back. You be good now . . . love you."

"Love you too Mummy."

The roads seemed eerily quiet on the twenty-minute drive to Sanglah, Bali's largest public hospital. Even the hospital car park was not fully occupied as is usual for any Sunday morning following the Saturday night road accidents. I parked on the south side of the parking lot, and walked briskly to the entrance of the U.G.D. (emergency room). The entrance was bustling and I attracted the usual attention from the locals, as being a 'white woman in uniform' I was out of context.

David soon appeared, fresh and cheerful as usual even though he had not slept. "Hi Kim, good to see you. We'll just wait here for a minute. Chrissie is on her way. You know Chrissie don't you? She's another Aussie nurse that lives over in Legian."

I knew Chrissie very well. We had once worked together at the International Clinic and Emergency Center (I.C.E.C). I was glad she was coming, she was a good nurse and it seemed like we were going to need as many skilled hands as we could get.

A hawker bearing trays of candies, drinks and cigarettes was taking advantage of the crowds that were starting to gather at the entrance of the Emergency Room. I found myself purchasing a packet of Sampoerna Lights, a local brand of clove-cured cigarettes. I had not smoked for years and I had never really been a serious smoker. Having one or two on a Saturday night was about my limit, but today I felt the need.

I offered one to David who politely refused.

"No thanks Kim, gave up."

"So did I but I think I might need these today. You sure you don't want one?"

He seemed to be looking at the packet as if he might. "No, no, I'm fine."

"Well you are a stronger man than me! . . . Look here comes Chrissie!"

2
Of Ducks and Doctors

We followed David in through the door of the emergency room and I braced myself for what I might see, but I needn't have. A few gurneys were occupied with what looked like patients with minor injuries. The floor was clean and it was generally quiet.

The emergency section of Sanglah was an impressive building for these parts. Built by the Japanese government in 1991, it consisted of the main emergency (triage) room, a medical treatment area, I.C.U., theatre suite, and radiology department connected to the upper level by a broad ramp that wound around in a large 'U' curve. There were about twenty or so one to four-bed rooms on the first floor. Unfortunately it had not been maintained as I am sure the Japanese Government would have liked it to have been, but this was a third world country and the Rupiah was no match for the mighty Yen.

Exiting through the back door we passed what appeared to be a medical records room that was already being converted into a communications center. A few expatriates and locals were exchanging notes and answering phones. The PLN and Telecommunication services were already making moves to install extra power lines and cables. David told me that we were going to the Melati wing; this was where most of the injured were being held.

I thought I knew the Sanglah hospital pretty well. I had been there enough times, either to collect tourists that had come to grief on the island and escort them to Singapore (or where ever they called home), or sometimes just to 'bed-sit'. Contrary to the Australian hospital system where relatives are given limited visiting rights, in this country the family is expected to stay, as well as perform most of the nursing duties for their relative. Feeding, washing, toileting and changing of bedclothes are all done by the family; if an expatriate was admitted as a patient they did not often have the extended family system to support them during their stay. Many are the times when the tight-knit expatriate community was called upon to bed-sit friends, as well as pay the bills.

We walked down what seemed like endless open corridors. There was no need for walls, it never got cold here, and a tin roof for protection against rain and sun are all that is needed. We passed labs, canteens, wards, storerooms, and the dialysis unit; these parts were new to me, this was the local economy section. The rusting old iron beds that lined the corridors and walls were reminiscent of something out of the 1930's. Most of the patients that would usually occupy this section could only afford the most basic care; some in fact would not be able to pay at all.

We hit a T-junction and a left-turn sign announced the Melati wing. All the other wards that I had seen had no more than four beds in a room. The Melati wing was a massive pavilion accommodating more than fifty odd beds at an initial guess.

I caught myself in a daze trying to comprehend what I saw. This was bad . . . this was very, very bad. In front of me stretched rows and rows of people scorched and burned, bones broken, battered and bruised.

"Right, now this is what we have to do . . ." David's voice broke my daze, and I found myself standing amongst a few other Westerners that David informed me were doctors who had come forward to volunteer.

"Unfortunately we can't do a hell of a lot without the consent of the hospital's administrators . . ."

"That's bloody ridiculous!" protested an austere looking middle-aged gentleman. He had to be a doctor . . . he just had that look! His accent was Australian, and he wore heavily rimmed glasses, with his shoulder length white hair pulled back into a neat ponytail. He would affectionately become known as 'Dr. Ponytail', for no one was going to remember anyone's name for very long on this day.

"I know . . . I know," David went on, "but we just can't. It could cause a political incident. It's illegal for foreign doctors to practice here, and they get pretty hot under the collar about it, isn't that right Kim?"

"Yeah . . . yeah that's right." I thought about it for a minute, I just couldn't comprehend the concern about political incidents when so much help was needed here, but I knew all too well the consequences of bucking the system. I had once been caught up in a very messy case and was charged for practicing without a license after assisting a man who had been fatally stabbed in the chest. The system can turn against you really quickly here, so I decided to stick with David's diplomatic concerns.

"All we can do is assist the local doc's and . . ." before David had finished Dr. Ponytail was protesting again.

"That's bullshit! Where are the doctors? Have a look around, I haven't seen one yet!" He was right. I saw nurses, lots of nurses, but not a doctor in sight.

David looked defeated "Okay, okay, Umm, I'll think of something . . . hmmm, I guess we could try and get consent, what do you think Kim?"

"Give it try, could take a couple of days though" I said, tongue in cheek.

"We'll give it go! We'll give it bloody good go lassie!" Ponytail held out his hand and introduced himself "David Marsh by the way". A firm kind handshake, I liked this guy. "Doctor" he said . . . "I suppose you guessed."

"Yep' it's tattooed all over your forehead! My name's Kim. I'm an R.N."

We had already started walking the long corridors back to the E.R. where I had previously seen the director of emergency services; he would be the man to address in this situation. The entourage consisted of David and myself, Dr. David "Ponytail" Marsh, Arthur (Art) an American emergency room doctor from the U.C.L.A. trauma center, Vijay a plastic surgeon from Perth, and John, a general surgeon from Wollongong. Chrissie had already been assigned to care for a severe burns case on the first floor of the E.R. building. When we reached the E.R. David pointed out an Indian lady who appeared to be assisting one of the local doctors. "That's Vijay's wife Priya, she's an anesthesiologist."

What a team, I thought! We couldn't have asked for a better lot!

I found the E.R. director standing wearily in the corner. "Permisi Pak (excuse me sir)." As I addressed him his face registered vague recognition. He had probably seen me before, and I him but neither of us could recall where or when and at this stage it didn't matter.

"I am Ibu Kim, I am here to ask for your help." I spoke softly and politely, for I knew aggression would get me absolutely nowhere.

"How can I help you Ibu?"

"These men behind me are doctors. They are here to help, but we would like your permission to do so."

"That's very kind of them Ibu, but there are rules here, protocols that have to be followed."

"I know sir, but this situation is not an ordinary one."

"That is true, that is true, but I am not the man that can give you that consent. I have superiors. You must find the hospital director."

"Thank you Pak, I will find him now."

We had spoken in Indonesian and Dr. Ponytail was the first to demand the outcome of the conversation.

"What'd he say, come on tell us what'd he say?"

"Find the hospital Director."

"Bloody typical! Hospital bureaucracy's the same all over the bloody world!"

I had once been introduced to the Director, and I knew that his office was on the first floor of the admin building. We were in luck, he was there with a few other men dressed in batik safari style shirts, as is customary for men in 'white collar' positions.

"Permisi Pak . . ." I lowered my shoulders as I entered his office so as to be polite. This was the only way to approach your superiors here, at least if you want to be heard.

The conversation went pretty much the same as it had in the E.R. This time we were passed off to the doctor in charge of the Melati wing.

Ponytail's patience was near expiring . . . back at the Melati wing and another déjà vu.

"You'll have to ask the doctor in charge of the E.R."

"We already did sir."

"Then you'll have to ask him again."

My own patience was also growing thin as Ponytail asked where we were going next.

"Back to the E.R."

"What for?!"

"Wish I knew!"

Someone called out for Vijay and he disappeared into the ward. We started out once again for the E.R. down endless corridors, we must have walked three kilometers already and I couldn't help thinking that we looked like a trail of ducks waddling at top speed. I thought out loud and Ponytail started to quack!

"Is that a quack I hear quacking?" I surprised myself with my own wit!

"Ooooh, that was fast, you'll keep girlie! I can see we are going to have fun with you today!"

Back at the E.R. I was not as politely received as I had been on my initial encounter with the emergency room doctor there.

"I think I told you already that you'll have to find the hospital Director! He is above me!"

"I did Pak, and the doctor in charge of Melati. We have been sent back to you." I stood my ground and I was not going to retreat.

There was silence; his eyes glanced around with his hands planted firmly on his hips. What was he thinking? What will he say? If he denies us Ponytail will lose it! . . . I'll lose it! There'll be a hell of a scene!

He drew a long breath and looked toward the ceiling "Terserah! (up to you!), do whatever you want, just do whatever you want!"

I turned to David and the doctors and raised my voice. "CAN SOMEONE WITNESS THAT PLEASE WE HAVE CONSENT! DID ANY ONE HEAR THAT? WE HAVE CONSENT!"

Davids face beamed "I heard it Kim, I heard it!"

David and I shook the doctor's hand and thanked him several times, but the look on his face told me that he was uneasy with his decision.

Ponytail was impatient. "Come on boys and girls let's get this show on the road!"

The duck brigade headed for the Melati wing once again, this time though, we ran.

Vijay arrived back at the Melati almost at the same time as we did. He pointed to a ward just west of the Melati as he spoke.

"Look guys, we've got to do something about this now, I mean RIGHT NOW. I've got at least six in there with compartment syndrome, if you don't cut them down NOW we're going to be losing fingers and feet left, right and center. If WE don't . . ."

Ponytail interrupted, "Its okay Vij we've got consent, we're all with you just tell us what to do."

"Well we'll need scalpels, lot's of scalpels, gloves, . . ." he went on.

Scalpels! Shit! Scalpels! . . . where would I find them in a ward like this? I asked one of the local nurses who started rummaging through the cupboards and came up with some razor blades, then I remembered my pack, it was still in the car.

By the time I got back with my bag, the nurse had found a box of sterile blades from I don't know where. The doctors all grabbed a hand full and stuffed them in their pockets, along with whatever else they could grab from my pack that I had up-turned on a vacant bench.

"I don't suppose I could trouble you for a scalpel holder?" It was Dr. Ponytail of course!

"Oh! Next you'll be asking for gowns, masks, hats and boots??" I said in jest.

"Well, that'd be nice!" He feigned an ever so feminine voice.

"Don't push your luck! On your bike Doc!"

3
The List

I was contemplating my next task, when David called out to me.

"Kim . . . over here! This is what we have to do next. We've got to get these people out of here! The planes should start coming in at about lunch time. We need lists, we have to get the worst out first. There's a girl over in the southern ICU, I promised her family we'd take her first. Go around to all the wards, all the rooms, make a list of all the ones you think should go first. Can you do it?"

"I'll try, but you'll have to tell me what kind of planes? How many stretchers? How many seated? How many ventilators? How many medics on board?"

"Okay I'll get on to Canberra. Oh and don't tell anyone what time the planes are coming. It hasn't been confirmed yet. You know how people get."

I knew better than to do something like that. Planes were always late! I always added two hours to the estimated time for plane arrivals when I was on a case, then it was a pleasant surprise if they came on time!

"One other thing Kim, we can only take Australians, Canadians, Brits and New Zealanders. These are the ones that come under the Commonwealth."

"What!!??"

"I know Kim, I know, but that's all we can do for now, I'm working on it though."

I would start the triage list over in the I.C.U. behind the E.R. assessing each patient and listing them in order of priority for the evacuation. By this time my phone was ringing incessantly. "Kim, do we need to give blood? Where do we go? What should we do? Is the equipment clean there?" Etc, etc.

Between the calls my thoughts turned to the immense task that I had been given. This was huge, me . . . ME! I'm doing THE LIST!

I had been trained in mass casualty triage, and had done lists on two other occasions. Both were mock-ups, both were staged bus accidents with twenty odd victims, class mates rolling around the floor with feigned injuries, some of them playing dead, but it would be nothing like this. Nothing could have prepared me for this! As I approached the double story E.R. building it loomed over me like a huge tidal wave, and I felt sure it would swallow me up. I couldn't go over it, I couldn't go under it, and I sure as hell couldn't swim fast enough to get away from it.

The I.C.U. (Intensive care unit) was very familiar to me. I had seen more than a few friends in and out of this unit. As I took off my shoes and donned a gown I was pleased to see a familiar face. Putu was one of the senior I.C.U. nurses and I had often marveled at the fact that it didn't seem to matter what time of day or night I had cause to visit this unit, Putu was always here.

He greeted me with his usual smile. "Hello Ibu."

"Pak Putu, it's good to see you! You're here again! How come you're always on duty?"

"We're all here today Ibu, too many patients."

"Yes, I suppose there are."

There was a silent pause as he opened the door to the main room. I sensed that he was looking at me and had trouble finding his words.

"I'm sorry Ibu, I'm so sorry about all this."

"Yes . . . yes Putu . . . so am I . . . so am I. So tell me what have you got here today?"

In the first bed was a sandy haired boy who was conscious but intubated (breathing through a tube) and on a ventilator. His hair was laced with soot, his skin glowed pink although he was not burned, and there were some flesh wounds on his neck and his abdomen. There was no name on his chart and so I introduced myself as I gently grasped his arm.

"Hi I'm Kim, I'm a nurse from the Australian medical team." He searched my eyes for more information. His expression was one of terror and confusion. He bit and chewed at the breathing tube protruding from between his teeth as if he were trying to say something. This kid had no bloody idea what was going on, or what had happened and so I offered a brief explanation. "There's been an explosion, many people have been hurt. Don't try to talk now, just squeeze my hand once for yes, two for no. Are you Australian?"

Yes.

"Are you from Perth?"

Two squeezes. No.

How the hell was I going to get an I.D. on this kid?

"Hold on there Sis . . ." it was Dr. Ponytail who had just entered the unit through the rear door.

"I might be able to help you with this, looks like this guy's fighting his tube. What's his oxygen saturation?"

"96% on room air." Putu answered and his English was much better than I thought it was.

"I'd say we whip it out boys, what d'ya think?" He addressed John, another Australian doctor who was standing behind him.

"I don't think it'll be a problem, let's give it a go." John agreed.

Putu prepared to extubate and no sooner had the tube been removed when the boy spat out his name in barely audible tones.

"Aden, my name is Aden!"

Aden would give me the most joy I would find today. He was a small victory in an endless battle-ground of failing souls. He was the first on my list.

An Indonesian man, Saiful lay in the second bed. He had shrapnel in his skull and was listed as a head injury. I thought of a musician called Saiful that used to play piano with Tony's band. Was it him? He could have most certainly been in Kuta on a Saturday night; there were several live music venues in that part of town. It was too hard to make any judgment on his identity as his face was swollen and disfigured. Saiful would have to stay; I could not list Indonesians, not yet any way.

In the third bed lay a young girl, and I would say from her development that she was not much more than fourteen years old. Her hair was a sandy blonde color, full of soot and it stood on end, her eye-brows seemed to be raised and her expression was as if she was facing a very strong wind. She had taken the full blast face on. This young girl had no obvious injuries, but I assumed that the massive compression force from the explosion had caused internal damage. She was unconscious and there was no reflex response. The ventilator diligently performed its duty and I suspected that this machine was her last link to life. She was listed as 'Miss X' and the only obvious identifying factor was an ornamental blue ring in her naval, for this reason she would become known as 'the girl with the blue belly button ring' and many pleas would be put forward for someone to claim this lost and lonely soul.

"What about this one?" I addressed Putu who was standing behind me.

"Doesn't look good Ibu, there's been no response since she came in, could be brain injury."

Shit! She's just a kid. She can't go on the list though, she won't make the flight.

I thanked Putu and left the unit. There was another I.C.U. on the far side of the car park and I would have to asses those patients next.

I wasn't more than a few paces along the corridor when I was stopped by one of the helpers who was with a tall middle aged man. He had a mop of white hair and a red face the sort men get from years of sun and beer.

"Kim can you help this man? He's looking for his teenage daughter."

The poor man was beside himself. "YOU GOTTA LET ME IN THERE! THEY WON'T LET ME IN! I GOTTA FIND MY GIRL!"

"Okay, okay, I'll get you in. There is one girl there, but she's not in a good way. She's about fourteen I'd say, sandy shoulder length hair, not quite five feet tall and slightly built. Does that sound like your daughter?"

"That sounds like her, it's gotta be her, I've been everywhere else, it's gotta be her! I don't care what she looks like for God's sakes just let me in!"

We walked back in to the unit and as he stood at the end of the bed he was silent and looked defeated. I waited for his verdict, then I would gently tell him that we were doing all that we could. He drew a deep breath and turned away.

"It's not her. That's not my girl."

"I'm sorry", there was silence as I escorted him out of the unit.

"WHERE DO I GO NOW? WHERE THE BLOODY HELL DO I GO NOW?" He walked away before I could offer any further suggestions. I thought of my own daughter. How would I feel? It was beyond my comprehension, I was sure I'd go stark raving bloody mad!

The second I.C.U. was on the southern side of the car park. It was generally used for more long-term cases. Today all four beds were occupied with victims of the previous night's explosion, one female and three males.

Ponytail had beaten me to it and was already scrawling notes on the bed sheet of the farther most bed. "About time you got here Sis." He had forgotten my name, and I was glad, as I had also forgotten his! He called me 'Sis', short for sister (as in nursing sister), and I called him 'Doc'.

"Listen Sis, will you come here and tell this guy that he needs to give these people more fluid?"

He was referring to the local doctor who had been left in charge of the unit. He looked young, all of twenty odd years old and completely out of his depth. I suspected that all the senior doctors were exhausted and that the juniors had been left to cope alone.

"Look at this, this guy's about ninety kilograms, he's a big bloke". The 'bloke' was known only as 'Mr. X' and had suffered multiple injuries; he was on a ventilator as were all other three patients in the unit.

"You gotta give him more fluids, here's the calculation." Dr. Ponytail was tapping his pen on the bed sheet where he had written the fluid replacement instructions for this patient. I relayed the message to the young doctor who seemed eternally grateful for the information and adjusted the intravenous drip rates accordingly.

Art, the doctor from the U.C.L.A. trauma center had found us and was gazing around the unit trying to put all this together in his head. He had come from one of the most advanced trauma centers in the world and it must have been tough for him to put his skills on to a different track and to make it all work in conditions like this.

"Look at this guy . . . they didn't even close him up. He must have a liver full of shrapnel, perhaps they'll go in again later," Art thought out loud. He was referring to a man in the second bed. His abdomen had been opened for surgery, packed with swabs and clamps, and left open.

Ponytail who was just leaving, made comment on Art's

observation as he passed us and headed for the door. "Bet you never see anything like that in L.A.! Looks like a bloody M.A.S.H. unit if you ask me! Gotta go! . . . See you 'round boys and girls."

Art pulled out a small digital camera and spoke to me softly so as not to be heard by the relatives who were sitting with the woman in the first bed. "Do you think it'll be okay to take some shots? They're just for my file, for teaching and stuff. I won't take the faces or anything".

"I'm sure it will be fine."

The camera made a zipping noise as Art took pictures of wounds, equipment and the primitive looking traction devices.

The ladies sitting with the only female in the unit spoke. "Are you the Australian doctors? Is the plane here?"

Art introduced himself, and explained his presence. They asked for his medical opinion and Art did a quick assessment of the patient's injuries. They searched for answers. Would their friend make it or wouldn't she? Art was kind and spoke gently but he was wiser than to give false hope where the chances were slim.

If the planes had ventilators I would put these patients on my list, if not they would have to stay. The phone rang and it was David.

"Kim I've got news that the first plane will take five stretcher cases, and then there'll be another one probably a Hercules with two stretchers and space for about twenty five walking wounded."

"What time?

"About three, but not confirmed yet."

"What about ventilators?"

"That's all I can tell you at this stage I'm afraid."

Shit! This job was getting really hard.

I made my way back to the E.R. where I would start assessing the patients on the first floor. At the bottom of the ramp I could see

David who was with a group of women that had come to volunteer as bed-sitters. He called out to me as I approached.

"Hi Kim! Just pop over here for a second can you?" David introduced me to the small group, although I was already well acquainted with most of the ladies there. "Kim will show you where the wards are, there's lots of people that don't have any one to sit with them. I suggest that those of you that can speak Indonesian sit with the Indonesian victims until their relatives arrive, those of you that don't can find a tourist to sit with. They'll need to be fanned as there's no air-conditioning in most of the rooms. Over to you Kim."

David disappeared, talking into his phone as he left. I split the small group up into twos and threes and told them how to find the wards. I had no time to escort them through the hospital as I still had much too much to do.

Lee, a good friend of mine followed me to the upper level.

"You can take this room if you like" I told her. "It looks like there are a couple of badly burned girls in there. I'll be back in a minute to do a full assessment."

The nurse's station was right next door so I decided to get what information that I could from them. The half a dozen or so nurses were chattering loudly about the previous night's experience and didn't seem to notice me jotting down the names that were on the white board.

Heading for the farthest room I almost bumped into Lee who was making a fast exit from her designated room. "I can't do it, I just can't do it!" The tears welled in her eyes. "I know I should but I just can't, I just can't see that sort of thing, can't you put me in admin or something? I'll do anything but I can't do this!"

Damn it! How could I have been so stupid! Why didn't I warn her? I should have told her what to expect! I should have let the squeamish ones go to desk jobs. I cursed my own ignorance and directed Lee to the communications room below.

I continued on my quest around the 'U' shaped upper level and I was not making good time. It was 11 o'clock already and I only had 5 names on my list. The lists would have to be ready by 1 o'clock. I would have had to move fast, I had to keep going.

These wards were where the extent of the horror really sank in, young people, all young people with horrific burns. In the first room were two girls. The farthest had been wearing a short skirt and a crossover strap top and these were the only parts that had been spared from the flames. Not many would have been wearing clothing enough on a balmy tropical evening to afford any protection from the searing heat.

I jotted down as many details as I could, trying to keep my handwriting legible. I started to note their injuries and faltered. Burns! Burns! Shit I had not done a burns case for years! I had certainly never worked in a burns unit. What were the percentages? What was the thickness? Burns information was somewhere in the back of my head filed under student nurse lectures over twenty years or so back. I could almost feel the rust snapping as the neurons struggled to shift! Rule of nines, rule of nines! . . . it was coming back to me, thank God for that! The rule of nines!!

9% for an arm, 9 % for front torso, 9% for back torso, 9 % for head . . . wait, kids were slightly different. God I hope I don't come across any kids! . . . 9% for leg etc. etc.

First degree was sunburn, second degree was red, swollen with blisters, skin loss and very painful, third degree was red to white and there was little or no pain as third degree burns destroyed the layer of nerves that lay just beneath the skin.

I found Chrissie in one of the far side rooms. "Hey Chrissie, what have you got?"

"Australian guy with burns, about 50% I guess."

"What thickness?"

"Hard to tell, most of them are already covered."

"Got plenty of fluid on board?"

"Yep, some guy with a ponytail just did a regime for me here on the sheet, but the line looks a bit dodgy, could be going into the tissues." Dr. Ponytail was carving his mark into the bed sheets of every patient that he assessed like some modern day medical 'Zorro'!

These patients should have had central lines, or an I.V. cut down at least. Putting a line in the peripheral (small) veins of the arm probably would not last, once their injuries started to swell the lines would pack up. At least they all had lines in I thought. Come to think of it, for the amount of people that must have come through the E.R. last night (about three hundred at least) they had done pretty well. Everyone had been treated in some fashion, all wounds had been covered, everyone had an intravenous line in, numerous operations had been performed and it was only about ten hours since the first patients arrived.

"You gotta name on this guy Chrissie?"

"Patrick, Patrick Hart."

"I'll put him on my list, he should be one of the first out. I'll keep you posted."

4
The Message

I stood for a breather in the annex of the building that led to the small car park connecting the E.R. building to the corridors that would once again lead me back to the Melati. To the left of me the other 'list' had been posted on the wall. Scrawled in thick black marking pen, half a dozen large sheets of paper listed the names of the dead or the missing. I perused for a moment, just to look, just to see and pray to God that I did not recognize any names that I saw there.

My phone signaled an in-coming message from my daughter. She'd probably just woken up, even though Adelaide was an hour or so ahead. She was not an early riser on Sundays, especially after a night out. Thank God she wasn't here in Bali. Thank God she wasn't in Kuta last night. I opened the message and read silently. "Mum, just saw news, said bomb in Kuta, said about 8 dead, 20 injured, you ok?"

Punching in the reply, my fingers felt clumsy on the tiny Motorola buttons. "News is rubbish!" I glanced up at the lists. "Could be 100 dead, 200 injured. I'm ok. No time 2 chat. Love u. Mum."

"Luv u 2 Mum, take care."

A little blue icon signaled that the message bank was full. I had better clear it out as there would be plenty more incoming messages today. I would check the messages first, to see that there was nothing important before I pressed the 'delete all' button. Scrolling down the list there was a message that I did not immediately recognize by the first few words. It read "Please come to . . ." I'd be better to open it and see what it was about.

OH MY GOD! The invitation! I had completely forgotten! "Please come to the opening of our new shop Sandpipers, cocktail party, Saturday October 12th, 9pm, casual dress. Regards Harumi."

OH MY LORD! The new shop was near the Sari club, she had

told me when she had seen me with her baby who had not been well. Oh my God! I hoped she was ok, I hoped everyone was okay! I would have known everyone there. I SHOULD HAVE BEEN THERE! Tony and I would probably have been leaving the party around the time the bomb exploded. My God! The hairs on the back of my neck and arms tingled and I had to sit for a while; I had to try to get a grasp on this. I had to think, to try to put it all in perspective. I wasn't just an outsider here, someone brought in to help tend the wounds, clear the carnage. I was in it . . . I was in this bloody mess!

I searched for a place to sit and was surprised to see a grubby corner of the steps that was unoccupied. It was a clear space, which was a good thing as I did not want to sit next to anyone. I did not want to answer the usual barrage of questions. "Hello missy, what your name? Where you from? Where you stay?" etc etc.

To the right of me a Christian fellowship group had already started to erect a makeshift canteen, handing out water and small packets of rice to passers by. I rummaged through my waist bag and found my cigarettes. I gingerly lit a cigarette and hoped that no one was watching. I hoped that none of the good Christian ladies would see that I smoked. Some of them had been my patients, or had brought their children to see me. What would they think if they saw me smoking? What the heck! I could be dead tomorrow! I could have been dead last night! Who gave a damn if I smoked? After a brief moment of introspection I stubbed out the remainder of the cigarette on the ground and started out for the wards once again. I had to keep going, I had to finish the list. As I walked my thoughts were still churning . . . Damn it I should have been there! What the hell would have happened? I should have been there!

It was busier now, the sun was high and the day was clear and bright. The light was almost blinding as the suns rays flashed and reflected off of windows, mirrors and parked cars. People crammed the corridors and foyers. The blood bank was packed with those that had come to donate their half a liter of 'liquid life'. Coming up to the last turn before the Melati a man was approaching me and seemed to be lost, unsure of where he was going, his eyes darting here and there. He was a short, graying man with a ruddy face and I felt compelled to ask if he needed assistance, or if he had lost someone. Perhaps I could give him some joy, match him up to one of the patients that I had seen.

"Excuse me Sir, can I help you, have you lost someone?"

"LOST SOMEONE? AM I LOOKING FOR SOMEONE? YES A WHOLE FUCKING FOOTBALL TEAM!! THE WHOLE FUCKING TEAM!! HALF OF THEM ARE IN THERE!" He pointed to the back of a white building that was just visible beyond Melati's southern limit. I knew this to be the back entrance to the morgue. "The rest I can't bloody well find, don't know where the bloody hell they all are. MY BOYS, ALL MY BOYS, WHERE THE FUCK ARE THEY!"

I was speechless and I had no answer for this man. Smart-ass I thought I was, thought I was being helpful, thought I could give him some guidance. I couldn't do a thing. I couldn't do a damn thing! He must have seen the look on my face, he must have seen that I was searching for words.

"Sorry love, I didn't mean to shout, I didn't mean it, it's just my boys, all my boys, it's just . . . oh shit, I don't know, I just don't know. One of em's just got married, gonna have a baby, what the hell do I tell her? What do I tell 'em all? . . . oh shit!" Tears welled in his eyes as he continued on his away.

Damn it! Damn those bastards! What had they done? What the hell had they done?

Back at the Melati the nurse's station just inside the entrance was crowded. Consulates, representatives of various nationalities, travel agents; they were all trying to find their people that had been drawn to 'paradise' for two weeks of 'heaven'. Another friend greeted me. It was Anna-Marie. She would be there for the Swedes. "Oh Kim this is terrible!"

"I know, tell me about it, it's a bloody mess . . . Sorry, look excuse me I've got to go."

"I know. I know you must be so busy."

I spotted David's tall lean figure across the way.

"David!"

"Oh Kim, glad you're here, how are the lists?"

"Getting there slowly."

Anna was behind me and addressed David and I. "When are the planes coming?"

"I'm sorry at this stage the planes are only for the Australians and the Commonwealth." David answered; he must have picked up on Anna's Swedish accent.

"What!? That's ridiculous!" Anna protested.

"I know but at this stage that's all we can do." David turned away as his phone was ringing again.

Anna looked toward me with shock and anger on her face. "Kim?"

"I'm sorry Anna that's the way it is right now but I'm working on it. There'll be other planes . . . I'm working on it I promise."

For a brief minute I hated David, I hated the selective rescue attempt that the Australian government had sanctioned. All I could do for the others was make empty promises, give them a little bit of hope.

David had finished talking on the telephone. "Now Kim how about the lists, the ones (patients) over in the I.C.U, have you got them down?"

"David I have to talk to you about this, the ones that go first . . ."

"Yes I know, but I've promised some of the families . . ."

"DAVID LISTEN TO ME! We have to take the ones that have a chance first! That's the way it is, that's what triage is about! You take the ones that you know you can help, those who still need urgent attention but we can help them. The ones that have a slim chance, I mean a really slim chance could take the space of someone that has a good chance if they are treated! This is the way to do it David, this is the way to get maximum survival!"

He scratched his head and drew a long sigh. His phone was ringing again. "Yes I suppose you are right, you're the expert. I'll let you get on with it." An expert I definitely was not and I was sure that David hated me for the cold hearted decisions that we were forced to make.

To the left of the entrance of the Melati was a smaller room designed to hold about two beds. Today it looked as if there were three or four and it had been set up as an emergency treatment area. The patients were all females, all young, and all badly burned. I could see Vijay and his wife working intensively on one of the victims. Her legs had been raised and her head lowered, her blood pressure had dropped and she was going into shock. Vijay looked intense as he held the oxygen mask tightly to her face while his wife Priya held on to her arm and looked as if she was trying to place an intravenous line.

Vijay was talking out loud to the girl, talking strength into her failing spirit. "Hang on there, come on, hold on just keep breathing. You're doing great . . . you're doing just fine!" When in actual fact she was not.

"We need central lines!" Vijay shouted. "There's the girl that speaks the local lingo, tell her to come here." He beckoned me with his eyes, his hands still working incessantly to breathe life into the girl.

"Sorry I forgot your name."

"Kim. What's up?"

"Can you get us central lines, the nurses don't understand me. Can you get some for us?"

"Do my best!"

These patients were in shock and all the smaller blood vessels would shut down concentrating the blood supply to the vital organs. A central line would put fluid directly in to the big vessels of the chest leading to the heart. Peripheral lines would just not be big enough in cases like this.

Where the hell would I get central lines? I could probably buy them at the hospital's supply locker, that's the way it was done here. When a patient was admitted you had to buy the equipment at the entrance of the hospital for the doctors to work with. I might not have enough cash as this sort of equipment was expensive and I'd need more than one.

It was crowded at the entrance to the E.R. How on earth was I going to get through this lot to the supply locker? It would be no use waiting around here, I was just wasting time. What about Putu in I.C.U.! Why didn't I think of this before? He'd have lines in the I.C.U.

Back at the I.C.U. Aden was now half sitting and sipping on water assisted by two expatriate helpers. He managed half a smile as I breezed passed his bed. I knew both of his helpers and so I called out as I passed by. "Hi girls, keep up the good work!"

"Do our best," they replied. "This boy says he's taking us out for a drink tonight!" The Australian humour was irrepressible.

"Oh really?" I smiled. "Not without me you're not, I saw him first!"

Putu led me to a small glass cabinet containing meager supplies. "What kind of lines do you want, Ibu?"

"Central lines in several different sizes" I replied.

He pulled one from the cupboard "You mean like this?"

"That'll do just fine, got any more?"

I could see the look on his face as he wondered who was going to pay for all this. As the nurse in charge of the unit he would have to account for all the equipment used.

"Give me two or three of each size, can you do it?"

"I think so Ibu."

"Thanks Putu, I'll replace these, I promise I'll come back, might not be today though!"

"That's okay Ibu, I believe you. You got to do your job too."

Back at the Melati I handed the lines to the nurses that were assisting Vijay. The girl was not doing much better but I had no time to stop, I had to keep going, it was half two already and I hadn't finished the list! There was no word on the planes yet so I should still have enough time to finish my task. The phone rang again and it was David. "Hi Kim, more news on the planes, . . . now its one plane with two stretchers and twenty five seated. There'll be another shortly after with twenty or so seated only."

"This is getting really tricky David! How am I supposed to do these lists?"

"You're doing a great job Kim, just carry on. Oh and it looks like the first should be here at six, but keep that under your belt."

"Six?!" Oh well at least that gave me more time as I'd have to re-shuffle the lists that I had made so far.

It was time to tackle the Melati wing. The name itself was an irony as Melati meant sweet jasmine flower and there was certainly no sweetness here today. The Melati consisted of two wards that ran parallel to each other. Old iron beds were filed closely down either side of each wall, and standing at the nurse's station the wards looked as if they went on forever. At the rear of the nurse's station was the separate room that Vijay had commandeered. There were no curtains, and faces were pressed up against the windows along all sides of the building, the walls were grimy and stained, and there was certainly no air-conditioning. Packed to beyond her normal capacity, the Melati was stifling. Helpers sat diligently fanning their patients, often in twos or threes and taking turns as their arms would soon tire. Starting down the right hall of the two wards, I listed the chosen patients one by one, detailing their names, nationality and nature of their wounds. Damn this was hard! Why'd I have to walk past some and not others? What was the 'Commonwealth' all about any way?

Nearing the archway connecting the two wards that would allow me to start working my way back to the entrance I started to hear the whispers, comments to which I paid little heed as I had too much else on my mind, I couldn't concern myself with anything else other than what was at hand. "Did you hear that Megawati's coming?" I heard one say to another. "That was nice" I thought. "That's nice . . . she should be here to comfort her countrymen at a time like this."

Within minutes the entrance was lined with military police in their navy blues, white hats and boots, they had ominous weapons slung over their shoulders and their pants too tight. Their pants were always too tight, and looked like they'd been painted on rather than stepped into! Someone blew a whistle and an official looking Indonesian gentleman started loudly addressing all the occupants of the ward. "Move aside, and stop what you are doing, move aside now and remain still! The lady President wishes to inspect the wards!" This was repeated in both Indonesian and English until all those concerned obeyed.

"What the hell?" I thought out loud. What the hell was going on? We couldn't stop working, not even for a minute, didn't she realize??

As she passed through she was hardly visible amid her entourage of military, ministers and body-guards. I thought how small she looked, so much smaller than she looked on camera.

Once permission was given for all to be 'at ease' I carried on with my mission. I passed a young German man who was attended by his friends and they called out as I walked by.

"Excuse me ma'am. Vat time are de planes coming?" The patient's companion enquired. How did they know who I was? The word had certainly got around that I was the 'list maker'!

"I am sorry" I said. "I am listing Australians only. I'm so sorry, it's just what I have to do right now."

"But our friend here, e's really bad. Look at him!"

Another time and another place I would have been alarmed at his injuries, but compared to what I had seen today, he was a minor concern. Ten percent burns maybe, a few fractured ribs, a broken arm perhaps.

"Look I tell you what, give me your names and I'll put you on another list. There'll be other planes, but I can't promise. You won't be the first ones out. There are many others much worse off, but we'll get you out somehow okay?"

Empty promises I thought . . . my nose was probably growing longer just like Pinocchio's curse! I jotted down the name of the patient and his companions. "Ingrid . . ., Hans . . ., Julian . . . Frank . . . Bert . . ." I was wondering how I was going to fulfill my promise, but at least I had given them some hope and they were grateful at least for that.

"Sankyou, sankyou zo much."

5
Slash and Burn

There were two other wards west of the Melati, the 'Kamboja' (Frangipani) and the 'Gadung'; combined they would have held at least as many patients as the Melati ward did. Clip board firmly in hand I started to pace slowly through the Kamboja ward. Vijay had left the girls in the Melati's makeshift emergency room and I could see him in the distance leaning over another patient, gently pushing on the mans scorched and swollen forearm. I heard him questioning the man as I approached.

"Does this hurt?"

"No."

"Can you move your fingers for me?"

"Hardly."

"Can you feel your fingers? Do you feel pins and needles or are they numb?"

"Don't feel much at all really, no, no . . ." The man was struggling to make even the slightest movement with his hand. "No I don't feel much at all."

"What you have sir is something we call compartment syndrome."

The man shrugged with half a smile. "Dutch to me Doc! What's it mean?"

Vijay's bedside manner was impeccable. He was softly spoken but firm and clear in everything that he said. What he was about to tell this man would not be easy, but he did not falter. The way he communicated was a form of art. Gently but surely he gained the patient's trust. He would have to play these people into his hands, get them to believe that what he was doing was for their own good for surely the 'escharotomy' that Vijay was about to perform would have sounded gruesome and bizarre to any layman with no knowledge of this procedure.

"This is what's happened and this is what we're going to do about it," he went on. "This arm of yours is quite badly burned . . . it's taken a real roasting in fact. Now, what happens when the flesh has been burned is that fluid leaks out of the cells and blood vessels and causes the area to swell. In some cases the swelling can be so severe that it restricts the blood flow to the fingers or toes, whichever the case may be. Once the circulation has been cut off, the tissue in the fingers or toes starts to die. If we don't fix this it could cause irreversible damage."

"You trying to tell me my fingers could drop off?"

"Yes, that's right I am. I'm afraid they could if we don't do something about it."

"So what are you going to do Doc?"

Vijay went on to explain the procedure as simply as he could. He would have to make longitudinal incisions in the forearm thereby allowing the extra fluid to leak out and relieve the pressure on the blood vessels that supplied the hand.

"Do what you gotta do Doc, I'm all yours," and he was. Vijay had reeled him in beautifully.

This man would feel little pain as the nerves that supplied the tissue beneath the skin had been damaged by the deep burn injury. Vijay made three to four inch long incisions to precisely the right depth along the forearm. A local nurse was handing out the gauze dressings from a large stainless steel canister that would soak up the straw colored fluid as it oozed out of the incisions. She looked on in amazement; she was more than likely completely puzzled as to what this doctor was doing. Her English language skills would be very basic and this young nurse would have no idea what this was all about. How bizarre she must think all this was? To be slicing open someone's arm that had already been sufficiently traumatized.

"There you go," Vijay said as he delicately wrapped a light bandage around to keep the gauze in place. "Those cuts might leave a bit of scar, but at least you'll still have your fingers!"

"Thanks Doc." The man looked relieved that the procedure was over. "You from around these parts Doc? You Balinese?"

"No, No I'm from Perth, my parents are Indian."

"Me too! From Perth I mean. I'm not Indian though as you can see!"

"Might catch you there one day, you take care now."

"Thanks Doc, thanks a million!"

Vijay knew that he would probably see most of these patients again as many of the victims were from Western Australia and Vijay was a plastic surgeon. These patients would all need extensive surgery and skin grafts. The constricted and disfiguring lesions of the burns' scars would need to be released and sculptured into functional and presentable flesh.

Turning to walk towards his next case Vijay saw me standing at the end of the bed, unaware that I had seen the whole procedure.

"Did you see that?" he gestured as we walked together through the ward. "That was a classic compartment syndrome. I've done more of these procedures today than I've done in my entire life! I must have done dozens already!"

"Yes, I did. Nice work Doc. These guys must be terrified though, at you coming at them with that scalpel. I know I would be!"

"Yes you're right, some are easier to convince than others. Then there's the language problem."

"Well if I can help with the local lingo just call."

"Thanks, but the Indonesians are not the problem. Most seem to speak some English and there's another local nurse that's been translating for me around here somewhere. It's all the others that are a bit of a worry. There must be every nationality on the globe here!"

Vijay was probably right. Asians and Europeans of every walk were here, Germans, Swedes, French, Koreans, Japanese, Singaporeans and more. Most it seemed though were Australians, there were even more Aussies than there were locals which actually made sense. I had since heard that the cause of the explosion was indeed a bomb, and that the Sari Club and Paddy's Bar had both been burned to the ground. The Sari Club did not encourage local patronage, which meant that the victims would have been primarily Australians, young Australians.

"Hey thanks for getting those central lines." Vijay said as he continued to assess each patient that we passed.

"No sweat, how are the girls?"

"Not good I'm afraid. Seems we get them over one crisis and then they plummet again. It doesn't look good."

Bastards! I thought again, cursing the perpetrators of this atrocity. Those Fucking bastards!

We pulled up at another bed and Vijay was already eyeing the man's feet. "Here we go again." He mumbled to himself.

I interrupted before Vijay started his spiel to the patient.

"Look Vijay I've got to keep going so I'll catch you around. If there's anything else you need just give me a hoy and I'll see what I can do."

What a stupid thing I had just said! Vijay had no more time to look for me than I had to look for him. Vijay must have been thinking the same thing and decided to take advantage of this chance meeting.

"Well while you're here what we really need is SSD antibiotic cream for the burns patients. Buckets of it, I mean that literally – we are going to need buckets of the stuff."

"Anything else?"

We conferred for a few minutes and came up with a list of a

dozen or so items that we thought were the most urgent of supplies that would be needed.

"That's all Doc?"

"Yes I think so, that's all for now anyway."

"Lunch maybe?" I asked knowing that he would have been working from daybreak without so much as a glass of water.

"Rain check on that thanks, maybe later."

I would call David and give him the list of medicines that we had compiled. If any of the planes had not yet left Darwin, they could bring supplies for us. Sourcing the medicines here would be a waste of time. I knew that the pharmacies always kept the very minimum of stock, and buckets of S.S.D. cream was not something that they would have just lying around.

David answered straight away as he always did. Every time that I had been with him, walking through the wards, meeting with relatives or officials he never once knocked back a call. Never had he said that he was too busy to talk, or told anyone not to bother him.

"Hi Kim, what's up?"

"We've put together a list of medicines here; things that they may be able to send from Darwin. Can I pass them on to you?"

"Sure can. Go ahead tell me what you need and I'll get on to it straight away."

"We'll need S.S.D. cream, buckets of it."

"Sorry what was that? F.F.D. creams?"

"S.S.D. Sierra, Sierra, Delta as in silver sulpha-diazine, and lots of it."

"You're breaking up Kim, I can't hear you. I'm just heading back to the Melati. Bring me the list and we'll take it from there."

As I entered the ward David approached and was looking weary although his pace had not slowed, even his shirt looked tired and was clinging to his chest in a large V shaped sweat stain. He sported what looked like a three-day growth and I thought that perhaps all the adrenaline had made his facial hair grow faster! David's long legs were striding out as quickly as ever. "Oh there you are Kim. Now what have you got for me?"

"A list of things that Vijay and I put together. We are really going to need this stuff. See if you can get them on the next planes can you?"

"Shouldn't be a problem Kim. We are trying to get all our people out tonight, but there'll be others left behind and they'll still need to be treated here. Oh by the way I have just had news that there will be a Qantas flight leaving for Sydney tonight at ten thirty. They have seats for thirty walking wounded. Any of the ones that can walk should discharge themselves and go to the airport and wait."

I was reminded again of the prejudice that I was bound to enforce. What if it was one of mine lying here, one of my children? What if it was Tony or myself? I had changed my nationality almost ten years ago when I had divorced my husband, had I not done so, I would have been forced to leave the country and possibly my children. Would we have been passed over? Left behind?

This was not the time to be thinking about 'what ifs'. "You've got a job to do Kim", I told myself, "now get on with it!"

There was another ward that I knew of behind the E.R. building. Tucked away behind the intensive care unit, it housed the only de-compression chamber on the island. You would have never have known it was there unless you were really trying to find it. The Ratna ward was a series of one, two and four bed-rooms that encircled a small courtyard garden.

It seemed that many of the rooms were occupied by patients that had not been injured by the blast; appendicectomys, diabetics, and a motor-cycle accident, nothing that would interest me. The bomb victims that I did find had relatively minor injuries. Minor burns, cuts and bruises; I would list them as walking wounded and give them the information about the Qantas flight.

On the far side of the horse-shoe shaped ward I recognized one of the helpers as being the French language teacher from the international school.

"Bonjour!" I said with a smile as I approached, for this was just about the only French word that I remembered from my old school days. The teacher must have known as she replied in English!

"Allo!" she replied. "I did not know zat you spoke French?"

"I don't! Used to though, I'm from the south of England and it was compulsory to learn French in the schools there. Who have you got in here?" I enquired as she led me into the single bedroom.

"Well Zis is Maya, she does not speak any English at all so I will 'elp you to translate."

The girl was not a native of France. She was dark, with large brown doe eyes, middle-eastern origins perhaps and she had suffered burns on both of her legs extending from just below the knee to the ankle, both of which had been bandaged so I could make no judgment as to the depth of the injury. One thing that alarmed me was that her toes had become dusky, swollen and cold to touch. Her ankles had puffed up like two big blower fish. Damn it! I thought, this could be another case for Vijay.

"Can you ask her to move her toes for me please?"

A brief confer and I had the answer that I did not want to hear. "She says she cannot."

"Does she feel her toes? Are they tingling or numb?"

"She says she feels nothing."

This did not look good and she would probably have to be cut down. I started to explain, just the way that Vijay had, what the situation was and what needed to be done, but it was not well received.

I did not need to wait for the English version to get the gist of what was being said.

"No! No! No! Je ne pas . . ."

She was not going to have the treatment; she flatly refused and was protesting loudly.

"I think I'd better get the doctor." I said to the teacher who was still trying to placate the patient between the screams and the curses.

Retreating from the bedside I noticed the bathroom that was for the use of the occupants of this room only. It was clean and did not have the rank smell of urine that reeked from the other public toilets that I had passed throughout the day. I thought I may as well take advantage! I relieved my self on the local style squat toilet and as I stood up and turned to do the dunk flush (bucket of water in the toilet bowl!) I noticed that my urine was dark orange. I had not taken any fluid since breakfast and I had been sweating like a pig. It was time for a break, time to look after me, but not until I brought Vijay back to see this girl. I excused myself and left the translator who had managed to calm the girl down somewhat although she was still sobbing and protesting bitterly.

As I headed for the exit via the nurses' station I could see one couple preparing to leave the ward already. The woman's arm was slung around her partners shoulder and she was limping and obviously in pain, but she was going and nothing would stop her now! They were going to get on that plane and that was all there was to it! I wondered how many would really get on the flight. Thirty seats was not a lot and I had heard that there were already long queues at the airport.

I found Vijay not far from where I had left him, and we marched once again down the endless corridors back to the Ratna ward. The muscles in my legs were starting to ache, and I silently thanked my running shoes for being so comfortable. My phone seemed to be ringing incessantly and I was thankful too that I had remembered to bring my hands-free cable that allowed me to talk without even taking the phone out of my pocket. As we approached the Ratna ward I could see several other walking wounded making a fast exit in the race to get to the airport.

The French girl was silent now and she was startled as we entered the room. Her eyes filled with fear as she began to protest again.

Vijay went into action and had her placated via the interpreter in less than a minute. He examined her feet, and it seemed that she had made miraculous progress in the short time that I had been away! She claimed to have full sensation in all her toes, and made convincing movements of all but the smallest of digits.

"Hmmm". Vijay was weighing up the situation, tossing for a decision. The patient was ranting and raving again as Vijay brought down his verdict. "Look, I think it will be okay, but if it gets any worse you'd better come and find me quickly, understood?" He was addressing the interpreter who was visibly pleased that she would not have to break any bad news to the girl.

She'd better not be faking I thought, it would cost her feet if she was! I thanked Vijay and apologized for my bad judgment.

"Don't feel bad about it," he replied. "She might have to be cut down eventually anyway. I'll catch you around . . . I've got to get back to those girls in Melati. It's really full on with them."

Vijay continued on his way and I stopped at the makeshift canteen that was now in full swing. I was amazed at how much had been organized in such a short time and how everyone had been catered for. There were packets of rice for the Indonesians; one box was labeled 'Halal' and was for the Muslims, one was labeled 'Nasi Bali' and would be for all of those that ate chicken or fish, and one was labeled 'Veg' for the vegetarians. Those that did not have a palate for the local cuisine could choose from cakes, bread and a variety of sandwiches donated by the gourmet cafes and hotel kitchens from around the island. Liquid refreshments consisted of a selection of fruit juice, water, coffee or tea.

I asked for an orange juice which I downed on the spot. "One more please . . . God that tastes good!"

"Thirsty work huh Kim?" the woman said as she poured another glass. Her name had escaped me, but I forgave myself for my shortcomings as there was much too much for me to remember today.

"I'd say so! Those corridors seem to get longer by the minute!" I replied.

As I drank I thought of David; if I was thirsty then he must be parched! I grabbed a bottle of water (the juice would be too hard to carry) a ham sandwich and a banana. I was not hungry myself; it must have been all the adrenaline as usually by this time by stomach would be protesting violently at not being fed. I looked at my watch. It was already four o'clock.

"How much?" I enquired, but there was no charge. All and sundry would be fed free of charge today, God bless the Christian women's fellowship!

I thought how funny I must have looked carrying the clipboard, food and refreshments as I made out for the corridors once again. Trying to walk as quickly as I could without the use of my arms had made me waddle!

David was sitting in the nurse's station of the Gadung ward talking with two other men. They were composed and fresh looking, neatly dressed and smart and as I got closer I noticed the color of their clothes . . . their T-shirts were pale army green, and they wore dog tags around their necks. The cavalry was here and that meant planes! Thank God I had finished the first of the lists!

"Ah Kim, just the person I wanted to see. This is Colonel Colin Lansky and Colonel Bradley Thornton, they're with the military."

"Nice to meet you," I set the food down on the bench and both men shook my hand. It was refreshing to smell the woody scent of their cologne, as the rest of us smelled pretty ordinary by now, including myself!

"I suppose you'll need these lists I have here?"

David replied before they could speak, as the two men obviously had absolutely no idea what I was talking about. "Actually Kim it looks like these boys will do their own lists. The military medics are working on it right now. I'm sorry. You've done a champion job though."

Part of me was totally deflated. I felt like a shriveled up, pathetic helium balloon, the kind that you see still floating around the house two days after a children's Birthday party. Another part of me however was pleased; my lists were still not finished, and what if I'd got it wrong? What if I'd forgotten someone or made a bad judgment call somewhere? It was better this way I'd thought, but what a waste of time, what a great big fat waste of time! There were so many other things that I could have been doing.

"Oh that's okay, it's great that these guys are here!" I replied, biting my lip and trying not to show how I really felt. "I'll get going then, plenty more to do out there. Oh by the way there's a sandwich on the bench for you David, you look like you need it!"

"Thanks Kim, Olga always said I was too skinny!" David said making reference to his wife. "Hey thanks for all of this Kim. I mean it. Thanks so much. You're an absolute saint!"

6
Robby's Story

The corridors were a constant stream of people by this time. Volunteers, people looking for friends and loved ones, as well as people who were just sight seeing. They had come to the hospital to get a close up view of the main attraction on a Sunday afternoon. I could pick the sight see'ers. They would stroll passed and their faces did not have the urgent look of those that were there for other reasons. They would nonchalantly walk through the wards, gaping mouths, occasionally pointing and screwing up their faces at the sight of something that shocked them. Some would gaze through windows or open doors. Some would even venture to the morgue to get front row seats for the 'gore and guts' show. What the hell were they doing here? This element of morbid human curiosity was unfathomable to me. Occasionally police or military from the local forces would pass through, but they were as powerless to control the situation as any one else. How would they know who was supposed to be here, and who was not?

The 'pecalang' (pronounced 'pechalang') presence was strong. The pecalang are the men from the local community that come out in force for any event that needed guarding or controlling in some way. Sometimes I cursed the way that they could close roads at a minute's notice (usually for a local temple ceremony), or how they seemed to have complete power over all and sundry and could not be questioned. The pecalang, it seemed, had more control than even the police or the military. In the event that force was needed (for disasters, community conflicts etc) they could call a 'turun banjar' (gathering of the villagers), in which every member of the community would take to the streets 'en masse'. Indeed it was the pecalang and the banjar (local community) that had done a good deal of rescue and fire control at ground zero.

Today it was comforting to see them. No one would cause a scene around these parts that was for sure. Most were big burly men, more Melanesian than Asian in stature. They wore the traditional pecalang garb; a black sarong, head scarf, and t-shirt, with a black and white checkered sash. Some sported a 'keris' (traditional sword) tucked in to the back of their waist band. The key members of the pecalang would even carry walky-talkies and could co-ordinate their movements via this network of radios.

I headed back towards the E.R. and was introduced to another Australian nurse, Jan.

"She's a phlepat . . . phlebtom . . . phlebtomotrist," said Karen, another friend who was here for the day.

"A phlebotomist!" Jan gave broad smile and corrected Karen's attempt at this tongue twister.

"Great!" I replied enthusiastically.

"What is that anyway?" Karen was puzzled at my excitement.

"A phlebotomist is someone that makes a living out of poking needles into people's veins!" I explained. Jan gave a hearty laugh and I was glad that she had not been offended by my simplified definition of her skills.

"Oh, well I'll leave you girls to it you seem to know what you're talking about anyway!" Karen hurried off, her task was equally huge as she was qualified in medical records and was trying to make some sense out of today's logistical nightmare.

I turned to Jan and explained that she should come with me to the upper level of the E.R. I knew that the I.V. lines there would almost certainly be failing by now.

"So a phlebotomist . . . that means you'll be a bit of a dab hand at putting in I.V. lines?" I was stating the obvious.

"Well I hope so!"

"What about I.V. cut-downs? Can you do those?"

"Yes I can, I haven't done a lot but I can do them." Jan seemed confident.

"Great, we'll go find Chrissie, she's another Australian nurse on the first floor. I think that her man will be the first you'll need to see."

An I.V. cut-down was the next best thing to a central line. Jan would be able to get a line into the deeper, larger veins of the arm. This would have to do until we could get central lines in all of the patients that needed them.

As we approached Chrissie's room I could see her standing outside the patient's door.

"Hey Chrissie, how's it going?"

"So so. This guy's urine output is down, and he wants to stand up to pee so I've let him."

Chrissie was standing in the doorway of the single bed-room so as to give Patrick some privacy. Chrissie had not closed the door as she would have to move fast if he had started to falter and fall and while this man could still stand, and was conscious and lucid, his injuries were grave. With burns to approximately 50% of his body, he was in little pain. This was an ominous sign.

Patrick was standing butt naked (any clothing would stick to his oozing flesh) facing the opposite wall of the room desperately trying to make water and just as I was about to introduce Jan a long fuzzy protuberance came across my right shoulder. It was a microphone!

"Excuse me," said a well spoken expatriate gentleman. "I'm sorry to interrupt, I'm from Island News Tonight, would you mind if we just did a bit of a shoot here?" The cameras were already starting to roll and spotlights flashed across my face as the camera man was trying to get a better angle of the room over my shoulder.

I was struck by a blind fury that would not be contained! "YES I

DO MIND! GET THE FUCK OUT OF HERE!!! GET THE FUCK OUT OF HERE RIGHT NOW!!!"

"But, but we're trying to give the world a story, people have a right to know what's going on you know!"

"AND WE ARE TRYING TO SAVE LIVES! GET THOSE FUCKING CAMERAS OFF NOW OR I'LL . . ."

I was about to get physical and the reporter sensed it. He made a hasty retreat, and he was fortunate not to encounter me for the rest of the day! Chrissie and Jan were gob-smacked! While I was certainly no angel, Chrissie had never before witnessed my temper unleashed, and the 'F' word was not one that I frequently used.

"Sorry . . . I'm sorry about that girls, but I'm not having this guy's naked roasted butt on national television! It's just not on!"

"Good on ya Kim! He bloody well deserved it anyway! How dare they?!" Chrissie was equally upset by the television crew.

I left the girls to their task and my phone rang AGAIN, it was my son, Krisna.

"Mummy, when are you coming home?"

"Sorry my love, it look's like it won't be for a while, tomorrow maybe."

"Aaww!"

"I'm sorry but that's the way it is. You'll have to spend the night at your Bapak's (father's) tonight."

"But why?"

"Because I said so!"

"I don't like it at Bapak's! There's no toys and he won't let us watch what we want on television AND we have to eat only vegetables!"

My ex-husband had recently turned an unprecedented page in his life, leaving a world of gambling, women and wild nights, for a new found faith in his religion, which demanded a much narrower lifestyle as well as a strict vegetarian diet.

"I know, I know but it's just for tonight. It's not really that bad."

"But if you're not coming home tonight how come you're not going to Singapore? How come we won't get presents?"

"I'm sorry Kris, there's so much to do here, just SO much to do. You'll have to go just this once. I'll call him now to pick you up, just do as you're told."

"Promise you'll be back tomorrow?"

"I promise. Off you go now, Mummy's got to go. Love you."

"Hmmmmm, okay."

I'd barely hung up the phone when a 'beep' signaled a missed call. It was David, I had better get back to him straight away.

"Hi Kim, can you meet me back at the Melati? I've got another job for you."

"I'll be there in five."

Exiting through the rear foyer I passed the lists of the deceased and missing once again. There were many more names than when I had last looked and rows of people had gathered to check the data. This was the last stop; this was where they all came after the wards, this is where silent prayers begged for exclusion from this list of the dead.

My phone rang again and the screen signalled an incoming call from my dear friend Shalima. Shalima was more senior in years than myself; a little younger than my mother I had guessed, but I had never been so blunt as to ask her age, for I knew this to be a well guarded secret. While we did not frequently meet, our friendship was solid. She was a colorful character and I'd loved to listen to the tales of her camaraderie, and she had enjoyed my company as one of the 'normal ones', inferring that there were more than a few loopy expatriate residents on the island (and she was right!). I hesitated to take the call, if there was one thing that Shalima liked to do it was talk! Oh, well, at least I could talk and walk and the corridors back to the Melati were long and so I pressed the answer button to receive the call.

"Hi Kim, I'm sorry to disturb you, I know how busy you must be. I've seen it all on the television. My God, who would ever have thought this would happen to our Bali?" Shalima's speech was impeccable, educated at the best of private girls' schools in Sydney's Northern suburbs, she had been drilled in poise and style.

"Yes it's not good that's for sure. Shalima I can't talk for long . . ."

"I know my dear, I wouldn't have called you but I think you're the best one to speak to at this stage." Her voice became sinister as she went on. "It's my nephew, Robby, I don't suppose you could look out for him? He's not really my nephew. It's my cousin's daughter's fiancé, but he's like family, you know how it is. He's a lovely boy, they're a lovely family. They just called me earlier on, they haven't heard from him all morning so I think they are starting to think the worst, you know."

"Oh . . . oh I see. Well I'll do whatever I can of course. I have the list here of most of the Australians at Sanglah, I'll go through them now. What's his full name?"

"Robby, or Robert actually, Robert Harper. He would be in his early twenties I guess, average build with brown hair. That's all I can tell you really."

"I'll give you a call straight away if I come up with something."

"Thank you Kim, I really want to help these people. You know how it is, it must be torture, you and I have both got sons. I can't imagine how this poor woman must feel." Neither could I. To lose a child in any situation was a tragedy. The horror of today's losses would be the not knowing. The hours, days, weeks, even months of clinging on to even the tiniest chance of a miracle. For some families bitter knowledge or sweet relief would come, but for others it never would.

As I entered the Melati, David was on the phone again, and he beckoned me closer from across the crowded foyer.

"Kim, I've got another big one for you I'm afraid. You up to it?"

"I'm all ears!"

"Well, we've been given orders to bring ALL the victims into the Melati wing. The military will then start evacuating from here, but we've got to bring everybody in first. I've got a couple of teams working to bring them in from the wards here, but there are several other hospitals around Denpasar that have patients. I need you to go to each one and bring all those guys in. What do you think? Can you go another round?"

"Ambulances?" I questioned.

"One of the Balinese guys, Agung Bagus, is working on it now."

"I'm on my way then and I'll keep you posted!"

"Great stuff Kim, that's fantastic!"

I would leave the hospital through the Southern exit, it would be quieter that way, and I could move faster. As I reached the corner, an unpleasant smell seemed to hang in the air and I could not place the odor as something that I recognized. I glanced over toward the back of the morgue and at first was unsure of what I saw. Squinting to focus on long white sheeting that was suspended a few feet above the ground I could see black lumps of wood that had been placed in longtitudinal rows beneath the canopy. What was this? Some strange ritual with which I was not familiar? Squinting to focus again I was smacked in the face with the reality of last nights event. The black charred lumps were bodies; rows and rows of bodies.

7
Catch Me If You Can

Scanning the car park, I could see no ambulances that were available for me as yet. I decided to take a taxi to Kasih Ibu, a hospital that was not more than five minutes drive from Sanglah. Once I was there I could commandeer one of their units to transport any patients that needed to be retrieved. As I sat in the car the driver was quiet, polite but not talkative, and I was glad, for I was not in the mood for idle chatter. These few quiet moments would give me the opportunity to go through my list and see if I could locate Robby. The light was getting dim but my handwriting was not difficult to read as I had written in large black letters, but I could find no Robbys or Roberts. As we turned the corner to the busy main road that would lead us to the small hospital car park the driver spoke.

"You a Doctor Ibu? You here to help?"

"No I'm a nurse." I kept my answer brief.

"This is a very bad thing Ibu, this thing that happen last night. It's a very bad thing."

"Yes, Pak. Yes it is."

I lifted my eyes to see that we were almost at our destination and I would not have to engage in small talk for very much longer.

"We lost drivers you know. Two of them I know, one my brother-in-law, one my friend."

"I'm sorry Pak, I'm so sorry. So many have been lost, too many. I'm sorry about your friends." I felt pangs of guilt for not having wanted to engage in conversation. Not wanting to listen to what this man had to say. We turned into the car park and I pulled out some loose notes from my waist bag.

"How much Pak?"

"No charge Ibu, you no pay, you helping people, you here to help."

I was taken aback by this man's gesture and I thanked him earnestly as I got out of the car.

I had previously visited this two-storey private hospital many times, and as I entered the lobby the receptionist seemed to recognize me and acknowledged my presence.

"Do you have any victims here from the Kuta bomb?" I enquired.

"Yes Ibu, second floor in the new intensive care section."

"Any one called Robert or Robby?"

She checked through a short list of names and shook her head. "No Ibu, but you check again upstairs, you look again there."

The several patients that were upstairs were Europeans, and had organized their own evacuation through private health insurance companies. Only one victim would be a stretcher case and apart from a broken leg and some minor flesh wounds his condition was relatively good. I was glad that everything was under control, and that I would not have to tell them that I could be of no assistance to them.

I would cab it back to Sanglah but unfortunately my next chauffeur was not as subdued, windows open and radio blaring he chattered constantly throughout the short ride. I was almost glad to be back at 'M.A.S.H. unit Sanglah!'

It was practically dark now, the local mosque was broadcasting its evening prayer call in long woeful tones, and the air was laced with the musky aroma of incense as the Hindus laid out small offerings of flowers and spices neatly arranged on small coconut leaf mats (canang).

Dr. Art Sorrel was making his way across the car park as I alighted from the taxi and he called out across the way.

"Hey Kim, wait up!"

"Hey Art, How's it going?"

"I feel just about as exhausted as you look!"

"Thanks, I won't take that personally!"

"Kim, I just wanted to check in with you about something, a guy I saw last night in Kuta, I'd really like to follow him up, but so far I haven't come across him, you've done more travelling than I have today and I thought you might have seen him. He'd lost both his legs below the knee, and had a piece of steel cable in his chest."

"And he was still alive!?"

"He was still talking to me last night. We did everything we could for him right there and then and I'd kinda like to make sure he's still doing okay."

"I can't say that I've seen anyone with those kind of injuries. Did you get a name on him?"

"No, I didn't think to get his name . . . I guess I was just too busy trying to do everything else."

"I bet you were! Look . . . If I see anyone that fits his description I'll be sure to get back to you, but I don't think his chances would have been good."

"Yes, you're right, it's just really bugging me that I could have been the last one to speak to him and I didn't even know his name. I'd really kinda like to talk to his family or something, you know?"

I knew exactly how Art was feeling; so many of us would witness the last minutes or hours of consciousness of the mortally wounded. We would hear their last words or hold their hands for the last time as they silently slipped away.

An armada of ambulances had started queuing at the south west end of the car park and I thought how they looked like a row of mechanical white horses waiting patiently to be commandeered. I was glad to see that the first in line was from the International Clinic and Emergency Center (I.C.E.C) and I was well acquainted with the crew. Nasir was the driver sporting his lime green, navy and reflecta-strip vest, he greeted me with a huge humble smile and almost a bow. I saluted him (as I often had in jest) and he laughed heartily. Nasir was a gentleman. The nurse on board was Salim and he was equally happy to have me on board.

"Good evening Ibu. It's good to see you again! You been here all day? You been working here at Sanglah?"

"Yes, yes Salim I have. Are you waiting for someone? Are you doing a pick-up here?"

"No Ibu. We've just been told to wait."

"Ah good, that means you must be waiting for me!"

"You sure Ibu? You looking for us?"

"Well I am now, come on lets go."

"What ever you say Ibu, where we going?"

"Wangaya hospital. You know it?"

There was a brief conflab between the two men, and it seemed that Nasir knew exactly where to go. The diesel engines of the Isuzu motor rattled to a start and we were on our way. The lights flashed and reflected off of walls and cars as we passed, not that this would get us anywhere any faster. It didn't seem that the local drivers were aware that an ambulance with flashing lights or sirens was in a hurry for a very good reason. In fact, some drivers would try to race or follow, and even intentionally get in the way.

"It's good to see you again Ibu. We haven't seen you for so long at the clinic."

"Well, I'll call by one day. I'm pretty busy now with my work, you know how it is!"

I was met at the lobby of the Wangaya hospital by a New Zealander, an expatriate called Martin.

"Hey, Kim, good to see you. You here to get these guys out?"

"You bet! What have you got here?"

"Well the worst is probably a guy that's lost both his legs, he's a bit agro though. Say's he doesn't want to go."

"We'll see!" I answered. I thought I might have found Art's patient, but in actual fact I had not. "Does he have any chest injuries?"

"No, just the legs I believe."

"Hmmm. What else have you got here?"

"A big American bloke, he's burned pretty bad."

"Okay, we'd better go check these guys out, Salim you bring the stretcher."

The patients at Wangaya hospital occupied a row of rooms on the far side of the foyer. The I.C.U. was to my left, and the other rooms to my right. I would start at the room farthest to my right, and the first patient I encountered was the amputee.

I introduced myself and explained my intentions but the patient was not happy.

"Just go away and leave me here will you! I'm not going anywhere! I'm not going back like this! I'm not going back without my legs! I'd rather bloody well die here!"

"I'm sorry Sir . . . but we will have to take you."

"JUST PISS OFF AND LEAVE ME ALONE! JUST PISS OFF WHY DON'T YOU!"

There was more to this man's story than initial encounters would allow to transpire. This man had lost much more than his own flesh; several of his friends were still missing, presumed dead. His feelings would be a turmoil of overwhelming guilt, immense sadness, and infuriating anger. This mire of conflicting emotion would rip and tear at his psyche, pushing him and so many others to the brink of insanity.

Anger was a normal part of the grieving process and I had been trained to deal with this. Sympathy would get me nowhere and I would have to be firm and empathetic and convince this man that we were here for his own good and that the services in Australia would be better equipped to assist him, but he was still not going to have it.

"I'M NOT BLOODY WELL GOING AND THAT'S THAT!"

I was in for a fight, and my next statement was probably uncalled for and almost cruel, but he would not challenge me again. "Well Sir, if you can get up and walk away, I'll leave you alone, but if you can't then you're coming with me!"

Salim looked shocked at my statement. "We take this one first Ibu?" He asked.

"Not yet, I want to check the others first."

In the next room was a Canadian man that did not look too bad at first glance. The nurses informed me that this patient had suffered from minor burns and so I did my usual introduction but when the man had tried to reply his words were completely garbled.

"Amenam ahh murmur nemdum." His attempts at speech were failing miserably. His brain and his mouth were just not connecting.

"Okay, its okay . . . don't try to talk, just let me have a look at you there." He had some deep burns on his right fore-arm and milder ones on both ankles; on closer examination I found that his fingers were swollen and cool.

"Can you move your fingers?"

"Nah nanana nah," he replied. Several more questions revealed that he had no movement in his right arm OR his right leg. He had suffered injury to the left side of his brain as well as possibly having a compartment syndrome of his right arm.

I turned to address Salim and we left the room to continue our conversation. "This man is worse than he looks Salim, we'll have to take him before the other guy. Did you notice his speech? Did you notice that he is paralyzed on the right side? His arm is pretty swollen too. We'd better get this guy to Sanglah ASAP. Get him on the stretcher and I'll go check out the I.C.U."

Martin, the volunteer from New Zealand, was already impatient for me to assess his patients. The man that particularly concerned him was referred to as the 'Big American'.

"Look Martin I've got to tell you something before we go in there, I'm afraid I can't take Americans."

"What?!"

"I know I feel pretty much the same way that you do, but I've been told to centralize all the Australians, and other citizens under the Commonwealth for the medical evacuation. There's nothing else I can do."

"But that's bloody ridiculous!"

"I know . . . I know, how do you think I feel?"

"But you gotta do something; there's gotta be some way that we can help this bloke. You can't leave him here that's for sure! At least come and have a look at him will ya?"

Martin led the way into the small three-bed intensive care unit, the American was in the first bed and at this stage I must admit, I did not have great expectations for this man's survival. He was conscious and although he could not speak, he acknowledged me with his eyes. I spoke softly and tried to comfort him as best I could. He appeared to be in little or no pain, and despite the fact that he had burns to almost every part of his body he seemed to be serene; there was almost a sense of resignation. He was not doped or mentally dulled in any way; he was alert and fully aware.

I glanced at the intravenous infusion flask only to see that it was dripping much too slowly. I checked through his chart which confirmed that his fluid replacement was indeed inadequate. I made a few quick calculations and instructed the nurse on duty as to the revised regime that I had made. She adjusted the drip rate accordingly, and did not question my presence. The old jacket and stethoscope had worked again!

In the second bed was an Indonesian woman and in the third a Singaporean man, both of whom needed their fluid replacement regimes revised. The Singaporean was sitting in his bed, and seemed to be coping well apart from some trauma to his left arm, and relatively minor burns.

Martin and I left the unit and paused just outside the exit. I was clutching for ideas that would give them something to work on, someway to get the 'Big American' out. "Does this man have any health or travel insurance Martin? We might be able to get him out privately if he does."

"I don't know, I don't think any of us have thought about it really." Martin replied.

"Okay, let's try to find out. Most people travel with some sort of insurance. You'll have to search through his documents, maybe have someone go to his hotel. Do you know where he was staying?"

"No, but we can find out. We have been communicating by getting him to point to letters and pictures on a piece of paper. I'm sure we'll be able to get that information some how or another."

"Right, see what you can get hold of, and then try to contact Jenny at International S.O.S. Assistance Company, Mario at Global Assistance or Richard Flax. One of them has surely got to be able to help us here."

After names and numbers were exchanged, I was informed by Salim that the Canadian gentleman was ready to go.

It was a short smooth ride back to the Sanglah emergency room, and our patient was becoming more and more frustrated at his attempts to speak. I took the time to try and give him a clearer picture of what had happened and where he would be going, but there were more questions that needed to be answered and he could not communicate. Perhaps he had lost someone? Perhaps he had been concerned about a friend, a wife, or traveling companion? His hands burned and bandaged so he could not even write and his words were locked inside a malfunctioning speech mechanism.

We unloaded the stretcher and I left the patient in the hands of the team that would assess him in the Sanglah E.R. before they transferred him to the Melati where all the other victims had started to gather.

I instructed Salim to return to Wangaya to collect the amputee. Salim would be able to handle him, he was a good nurse and there was no need for me to go along. My next port of call would be the Military hospital (otherwise known as the R.S.A.D.). I could see another I.C.E.C. ambulance at the head of the queue, but much to my disappointment it had already been spoken for. Next in line was a military unit, which was bigger, almost a minibus in size. It was not nearly as well equipped as the I.C.E.C. units, but it would have to do for the time being. The lights flashed and the siren made a strange whining noise as if it were running on half-charged batteries! The crew was polite and friendly and we soon became acquainted. The usual comments and apologies were made in reference to the previous night's events. Even as a veteran of this country I still found it touching that each Indonesian that I spoke to, regardless of ethnic or religious background, apologized for what had happened. It was as if each felt some responsibility for what had occurred or perhaps felt that they should have in some way have been able to stop it.

The phone rang and it was a gentleman who was assisting the victims that were being treated at the Prima Medika hospital. One of the patients was his daughter.

"Oh Hello, Kim is it?"

"Yes that's correct, what can I do for you?"

"Ron's my name, and I was given your name by the Australian Consul, he said you were doing the pick-up for all the people being held at the other hospitals; that you would come and get us and we would be going to the Melati ward in the big hospital so we could get on a plane?"

"Yes that's right Ron. I'm on my way to the military hospital right now so you'll be next. How many have you got there anyway?"

"Three girls, two are not that bad, one has a bit of a head injury, she's had a CAT scan and the doctor says it doesn't look too bad and that she's stable. We're alright here really I just wondered what time you'd be here and to make sure that we weren't forgotten."

"Won't forget you I promise. It'll probably be an hour or so but I will definitely be there."

"Okay love, we'll see you then."

The military hospital was only a short drive but I took advantage of the few quiet minutes to call the other hospitals that might have taken patients from last night's explosion. Directory assistance got all the numbers right for a change and I called each one, the Puri Rahardja hospital, the Dharma Yadnya, Surya Husada and Manuaba private hospitals but none had any 'tamu' (foreign guest) occupants and I was glad. This meant that after the R.S.A.D., the Prima Medika would be my last run, and I was feeling, to say the least, a little weary.

8
Small Wounds Run Deep

The green army minibus pulled up at the entrance of the R.S.A.D. and I was greeted once again by humble smiles. This hospital was not familiar to me, I suppose because I had little cause to ever be there. The R.S.A.D. was generally for military personnel and their families, not for tourists or expatriates.

The nurse in the E.R. showed me the list of the victims that had been admitted earlier in the day, and it seemed as if I had about half a dozen people to move. The patients were all centralized in one ward which consisted of several three and four-bed rooms. The usual teams of resident expatriates were there to bed sit, the faces of whom I recognized, but the names had once again escaped me! One room was occupied with Japanese patients and their consulate seemed to have everything under control. Another room had a small group of Australians but not all were in beds. Some, although suffering from minor injuries, were sitting next to the beds, comforting those that were more severely affected.

All of the patients except for one would be able to sit in an ambulance, and could walk or sit in wheelchairs at the airport. There was no sense in sending them to the Melati, they could take the military van out to the airport and wait for assistance there. They piled into the Ambulance one by one, limping and hopping; one boy had to hoist himself from his wheel chair onto the ambulance bench seat wincing with pain as he did so. I explained where they were going and that there would be wheelchairs and people to assist them at the airport. I wished them luck, and thought what a sorry lot they looked. They were all young boys, Adrian, Jason, Adam, and Dayle, they didn't look much more than teenagers. They would all do well, none were severely injured and as I pulled down the rear hatch of the van I wondered who they'd left behind, who would not be going home and how their young lives had been so horribly marred by the memories of what had started out as two weeks of partying in 'paradise'.

I stopped to peruse the list of patients at the admissions desk one more time before I made my way back to the ward, but there were no other patients apart from the ones that I had already seen. There were no 'Robby's' and no 'Roberts'. Shalima's nephew was not here either.

I walked back to the ward through several maze-like corridors to find the only two Australian victims that remained with another man who had elected to take care of them. Only one of the two patients, Stewart, was bed-ridden. He was a big sturdy man, and was probably in his late twenties or early thirties; I thought by his build that he might have been a rugby player. He was conscious and no severe injuries were initially apparent. I introduced myself to the patient and his companions, and as I did so I noticed that the patient was lying flat with his head supported on either side by two pillows. He did not make any attempt to look at me or turn his head to meet my eyes when I spoke, and I initially thought he may have fractured his spine, or sustained some other injury that might have caused him not to move.

The older of the two gentlemen pulled me aside and suggested that we take a short walk. He introduced himself as a G.P. from Australia and what he had to say made it clear that moving this man was not going to be an easy task!

"Look Kim, when you go back in there be very careful with this fellow. He doesn't look too bad, and until now he has been okay. When you examine him, have a look at his neck, just over towards the left side. There's a small wound that looks benign enough, but I believe there could be a bit of a problem there. I've had a listen to his neck, and there is an untoward sound that I think is coming from one of the major (blood) vessels. There's probably something stuck there, a piece of shrapnel and it's sitting dangerously close to the carotid. One wrong move and this guy could be a gonner!"

"Good Lord! You're pretty sure about this then?"

"Yes I'm afraid so."

"Hmmm. Well I'll have a quick look but I'm sure that you're much more skilled than I am at this sort of thing."

The patient's name was Stewart Alastair and he seemed to be in good spirits all considered.

"Okay Stewart, lets have a look at you there, the good doctor here says you've got a bit of a problem with your neck. Just lie still and I'll come on that side and have a quick look at you."

There was a small laceration on the left side of his neck, only about a centimeter long and the innocent appearance of this wound belied its sinister implications. One wrong move and it was all over. The carotid artery would carry tens of liters of blood to the brain every minute and if she blew it would be a disaster. I had seen a carotid bleed once before, the pressure from the blood in this vessel was so strong it could change the color of the ceiling to blood red in seconds.

"Hmmm, looks like we have a problem Houston." I tried to keep the mood light, and Stewart gave half a smile. "We'll get you out of here don't worry. I'll have to get another ambulance though, one with better equipment. The ones they have here won't have what I'll need. I'll be back in about half an hour. Wait for me?"

Stewart smiled again. "Well I'm not going anywhere!"

"Goodo, I'll see you in a short while then."

The doctor walked with me to the exit, we discussed the task at hand and I decided to try and enroll his expertise for the journey.

"Look Doc, I'm going to get another ambulance, I'll need more

Continue to page 89

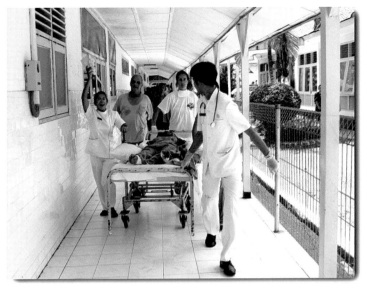

"Mark Keatinge assists Sanglah staff to transport one of the victims".

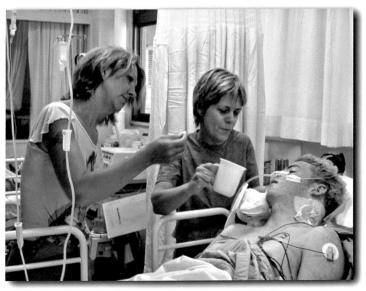

"Verna and Tracy assisting one of the victims in the I.C.U."

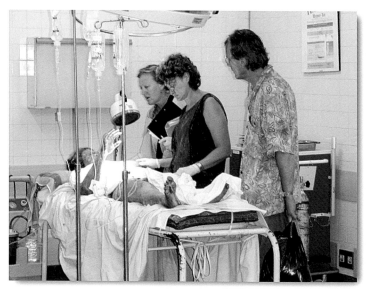

"Julie and friends treat a patient in the Sanglah emergency room."

"The communications room manned by volunteers at Sanglah Hospital."

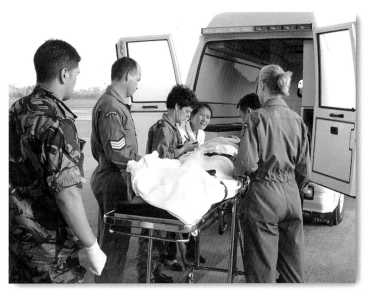

"Military medics at Ngurah Rai Denpasar Airport."

"Big green angel at Ngurah Rai Denpasar airport."

"Floral tributes outside of a shop adjacent to the Sari Club."

"The remains of Paddy's Bar (right)"

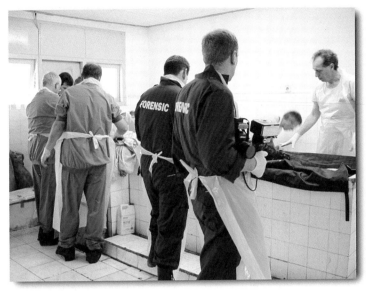

"Forensic teams work at the Sanglah Morgue."

"Corpses lay under plastic and bags of ice behind the morgue."

"Coffins stacked outside the morgue."

"The long, open corridors of Sanglah hospital."

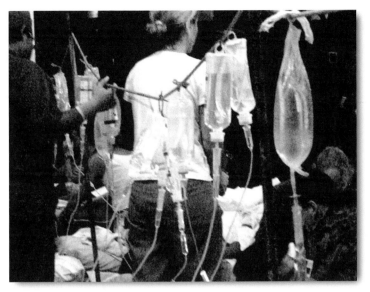

"Preparing patients for evacuation at the airport."

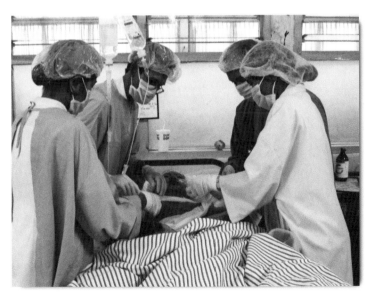

"Performing emergency procedures at the bedside - Sanglah Hospital."

"Emergency supply tents outside Sanglah's emergency department."

"Preparing for medical evacuation, Ngurah Rai Airport."

equipment than they have here, at least a proper stretcher and a neck collar. Do you think you could ride with us, just in case something happens and we have to intubate (put a breathing tube down) or something?"

He looked at the ground as we walked towards the exit and drew a long, purposeful sigh before he gave his answer. "Look, to be perfectly honest with you, if he really does blow it, there's not a damn thing that we can do, you'll just have to be careful, really careful."

"That I will doc . . . that I will!"

The hospital staff were kind enough to drop me back at the Sanglah hospital and during the short ride the phone rang, it was Ron at the Prima Medika hospital. I took the call and before he could speak I was apologizing for not yet having been to see the girls that were there.

"Oh don't worry love, that's why I was calling you. I've been for a walk over to the big hospital to have a gander at the Melati ward where we are supposed to go. To be honest we are better off here, we've got air conditioning and a nice room, and I think we'll stay until the planes arrive."

That sounded like good logic to me. I would tell David and the military boys that the girls needed to be collected from the Prima Medika.

Back at Sanglah I was pleased to see that another one of the better I.C.E.C. units was waiting at the front of the ambulance line up, and this time it was not spoken for. This ambulance was the smaller of the I.C.E.C. units; a late model Mercedes Benz van and she rode as smooth as silk. With her next patient the European independent wheel suspension would be her greatest asset. The roads in Bali can be rough in places, and this truck would ride them all with ease.

Tono was the driver and the nurse was Ketut. I explained our situation to the nurse on the ten minute ride back to the R.S.A.D and he prepared several sizes of cervical neck collar that we would need to stop any undue movement of Stewart's neck. The ambulance cruised into the R.S.A.D. emergency entrance, and Ketut unloaded the stretcher while I went ahead to fit the collar.

Back at the bedside I slid my hand carefully under Stewart's neck grazing my hand on several pieces of glass that were still on the under-sheet. I gently pulled the collar back through, then fitted Stewart's bearded jaw into the chin rest, and fastened the collar. My heart was racing as I tried not to convey any of my fears and I said a silent prayer as Stewart looked up and gave me another smile. Ketut arrived with the stretcher and we meticulously rolled our patient onto the back-board then lifted him in unison onto the stretcher. Another prayer . . . another smile . . . so far so good!

The 'knock-down' style stretcher slid easily into the van, as we fare welled the doctor. I wanted to compliment him on his tremendous skill. Many others would surely have missed the seriousness of this man's injury but the ambulance was pulling away before I could find the words.

Stewart's friend Nathan would ride with us and stay with Stewart for the rest of his journey. Both men looked exhausted and Nathan appeared as if he would doze off in the air-conditioned comfort of the van. There would be no point at all taking Stewart back to the Melati. I would take him straight to the I.C.E.C clinic which was on the way to the airport, and we could get an x-ray done there.

The twenty-minute drive to the I.C.E.C. went without a hitch. We eased the stretcher out of the van, and Stewart was wheeled straight into the x-ray room. I briefly explained to the technician that we would need a picture of the neck from front and side view, and that the patient could not be moved. The neck collar remained in place, as it was the x-ray friendly kind, and would not interfere with the film.

I offered Nathan a cup of tea and apologized to Stewart for excluding him from the offer. From now on he would have to fast in preparation for any surgery, which he was certain to have in Australia. Nathan and I left Stewart with the nurse and the radiologist while the films were taken and Nathan made himself comfortable in the waiting area while I went to the staff kitchen. The nurses on duty greeted me warmly although I expected that they were all too tired to do much more than this. The medical center was situated only a few kilometers from the blast and the I.C.E.C. along with the neighboring International S.O.S. Assistance center had been the first stop for many of the victims as they fled from the explosion and all staff would have been called in to assist. When I returned to the waiting area Nathan was sleeping soundly on the chair, and I thought better of waking him from his slumber.

The 'No entry' light to the x-ray room had been switched off and the technician appeared at the door. He beckoned me to the viewing booth, and our suspicions were confirmed. A piece of shrapnel, probably glass as it did not have the well defined appearance that you would have expected to see if the object had been metal, was positioned exactly where the doctor had said it was, right next to the carotid artery.

I would inform David who would organize for the military medics to collect Stewart on the way to the airport. David was all ears as I explained the situation, he promised that the medics would probably be there within the hour. I relayed the message to Stewart, and wished him luck for the rest of his journey.

As I sat outside on the low surrounding wall waiting for a taxi I took a few quiet moments to reflect. There was a light breeze and the streets seemed almost deserted apart from the occasional minibus or military truck heading towards the airport. Today had been incomprehensible, unfathomable. Why here? Why us? What conflict did we have that would warrant this magnitude of aggression? What was the motive? What the hell did these people think they were going to achieve?

The taxi arrived and as we drove back towards Denpasar I made several phone calls that would excuse me from any conversation with the driver. The first call would be to Shalima, and I wished I had better news for her but until now I had found no 'Robbys', 'Roberts' or 'Harpers'.

"Hi Shalimar, are you still awake?"

"Yes Kim, go ahead, I'd like to think that you had good news for me but my gut feeling says that you haven't." Shalima was intuitive to the point of being almost psychic and I had witnessed her talent on many an occasion.

"Well, you're right again of course Shali, I haven't found Robby yet, but I'll keep trying. There are still a few smaller village hospitals and clinics and you never know."

"Thanks my dear. I know how you feel. I know you're feeling just like I am. If it was one of our boys you'd go to the ends of the earth, and it must be so frustrating for his family not to be here, not be able to do anything themselves."

"Hmmm, I can't imagine how they must feel, I'll keep looking, and I'll let you know if I come up with anything. I'd better go now I still have a few more things to do."

"Goodnight my dear and God bless you for all that you've done."

I sent a message to David enquiring his whereabouts, as I would need to give him the report of all the people that I had sent to the airport. David answered almost immediately, he was at the Melati and I agreed to meet him there. The taxi pulled into the car park and I noticed that my old Peugeot was parked not far away. I wondered if she would start for me when I was ready to head for home, or whether she would be as temperamental as the French can sometimes be and refuse the favour! I hoped I would soon find out. One more visit to the Melati and my mission would finally be over.

As I walked the long corridors for one last time I was aware that my pace had slowed. My legs ached like they had never ached before; the joints, and pistons, turbines and coils were in desperate need of attention. This old cruiser was about to collapse! "Just one more lap", I thought to myself. One more round and I would be on the home run.

The Melati ward was packed with far more people than should ever have been allowed beneath her rafters. Wall-to-wall people were standing, sitting, lying in any position that they could find tolerable. The heat was more than stifling. The atmosphere was one of expectation, and as I bumped from body to body the Germans that were on my 'other list' called out to me. "Zank you Miss, zank you Miss ze plane is coming for us, zankyou zo much!"

I was puzzled by their gesture of appreciation but I was too tired to argue the point or make further enquiry. All I could do was raise a hand and smile and hope that someone else had not made them false promises as I had done earlier in the day. I was almost back at the exit and I had not yet found David. Another familiar face was just ahead, Mark, a long time expatriate of Sanur, greeted me and made comment on the human sardine situation.

"Hey Mark, good to see you."

"You too Kim, you're looking a bit weary there, and your back pack looks a bit deflated as well!" Mark was making reference to my old red bag that was still lying empty and crumpled on the bench.

"Yeh! It looks a bit like I feel right now!" I scooped up the empty bag and was about to make my way along when Mark spoke again.

"Hey great news about the planes, yeah?" Mark obviously knew more than I did. I had heard nothing as for the past few hours I had been confined to the back seat of an ambulance.

"Are they here?" I asked.

"Yep, apparently, and they've lifted the regulation on Aussies only!"

"What?! That's fantastic!" I was all ears as Mark went on to explain that the military medics had made the decision to air-lift all the foreigners. The Australians were now willing to assist all nationalities; however the Indonesian Government would not allow it's nationals to be evacuated. At least we would get the other nationalities out, perhaps the Indonesians would be able to go tomorrow, or perhaps they would be taken to Jakarta where they may have better burn care facilities.

I could see David through the crowd so I bade Mark farewell and made out for the other side of the nurse's station before David had a chance to disappear into the sea of people.

David was looking as wilted as I felt, although his pace was not slowing, and he would not leave the Melati for many hours to come. I handed him the list of persons that had been sent to the airport, and reminded him about Stewart, as well as Ron and the girls at Prima Medika.

"I'm done now David, I think I'm done." I declared as I signed off my duties for the day.

"Okay Kim, I'll get someone to take over from you. Which hospitals have you cleared and which ones are not done yet?"

"They're all cleared . . . all the hospitals in Denpasar anyway."

"All of them?" David looked surprised.

"As far as I know, but I've only got the Aussies and the other ones that you told me I could take. Mark says it's different now . . . he says we're taking everyone except the locals?"

"Yep that's right! It's great isn't it?" David was as perky as always!

"Fantastic . . . But I don't know if I can go another round! I don't think I can go out there again to get the ones I left."

"Don't worry I'll get the military boys on it. You've done a great job. Go and get yourself some rest, you deserve it!"

"Thanks! What about yourself?"

"Oh, I'll be here for a while yet, you just go, we'll be fine now."

I made for the southern exit, past the ominous white sheeting that had now been dropped to cover the corpses that lay below. The odor that had previously been a scant waft of unpleasantness was now a putrid stench of death. I turned the corner to head toward the car park, passed the southern intensive care unit and the coronary care ward. Standing at the last building before the car park exit I could see the familiar silhouette of Dr. David 'Ponytail' Marsh, with his arm around a woman that was obviously his mate and his mentor. She was his perfect match, and even on this less than glamorous evening she was a picture of style and grace. Her hair was cut in a neat bob and her spectacles were a fashion statement.

Dr. Marsh gave a broad smile as I approached and he greeted me with his usual camaraderie.

"Ah there you are Sis, thought you'd got lost! Where've you been all this time?"

"Oh you know, there's more than one man in my life, so I've got to travel fast!"

Both the doctor and his lady laughed heartily and David made the introductions.

"This is my wife and definitely my better half, Claire . . . and Claire this is . . . I've done it, I knew I would, I can't remember!"

"That's okay, I'm glad I'm not the only one that's amnesic, my name's Kim."

Claire grasped my hand in a long sincere handshake. "I'm very pleased to meet you Kim. I suppose it's been a long day for you as well."

"Yes, yes it certainly has. Not exactly what I was planning to do with my Sunday that's for sure!"

"No I'm sure it wasn't! David and I had quite a day planned but I suppose our massage will have to wait!"

"Hmmm a massage sounds good I think my legs are starting to buckle at the knees!" I replied.

Dr. Marsh was obviously feeling the same as he rubbed the small of his back and winced as if he was in pain. "Me too Sis, this little black duck has seen better days I can tell you, I'm done for. I haven't done a shift this long since I was an intern and that's a few years ago!"

I looked at my watch; it was midnight, eighteen long hours since we had started pacing the wards.

"You on your way home then kiddo?" the doctor enquired.

"I certainly hope so, and you?"

"Oh yes, I've got this here lady to keep happy, and who knows I might even get some sleep!" Another short burst of laughter and we shook hands once again to farewells and vows that we would all meet again to solidify the bonds that we had made on this day.

The old Peugeot must have sensed that I did not have the energy or the inclination to coax her into starting and the engine turned over beautifully on the first attempt . . . The air conditioner and the tape deck however were not so obliging. No matter as the evening was cool and I could listen to the radio instead. It would be pleasant to breeze laced with the scent of the incense, the smell of the clove cigarettes as I passed small gatherings of night watchmen, and the aroma of the satay as the carts took their last orders on the sidewalks. I wanted to inhale the life, to feel alive.

The radio crackled as I searched for the easy listening station on the dial. The D.J. must somehow have known the way I felt, the mood of the moment, as a song that I had not previously heard filled me with it's soulful tones.

"Feeling tired, by the fire . . . the long day is over; The wind is gone, asleep at dawn . . . the embers burn on; No reprise, the sun will rise . . . the long day is over . . .". Norah Jones was singing me home.

I pulled into the drive and the dogs nearly turned themselves inside out when I entered the yard. The house was dark and there was not a soul around. There were four things I desperately needed: a drink, a pee, a shower and bed, in that order. I drank almost a liter of ice cold milk, relieved myself in the downstairs bathroom (only to find that my urine was by this time as black as strong English breakfast tea!), showered scrubbing every inch of flesh from head to toe, and collapsed on a bed that I swore was heaven.

9

What God Has Joined Together
Let No Man Put Asunder
Monday October 14th, 06.00 hrs

Despite the previous day's marathon, my eyes were already open when the sun's first rays crept through the bedroom window. I drew in a deep breath and arched my back, stretching every aching muscle, silently thanking the dawn that yesterday with all its calamities was over. I tried to collect a few scattered thoughts and planned what I would do with the morning. I even had visions of the day being somewhat normal or ordinary, and that what had happened was done and gone or perhaps not nearly as bad as I had remembered it had been. There was almost a sense of surrealism.

Any silence or serenity was soon shattered by the sound of the telephone; it was only six thirty a.m., who on earth could it be? Several calls followed one after the other, and the questions were the same. People still wanted to donate blood, give their time and their skills to help out in any way they could. Hadn't anyone told them it was all over, didn't they know they were a day too late? There was no point in staying in bed as I could see there would be no sleeping in on this morning. The phone rang again and it was David from the consulate. Why had he woken so early? He would have gone to bed even later than I did! I took the call still in half a waking daze, imagining all sorts of atrocities that could have occurred again, more bombs, more explosions, and that the corridors of Sanglah were once again beckoning one and all.

"Good morning David, what can I do for you?"

"Morning Kim, hope I didn't wake you?" David was as cheery as ever.

"Not at all, thought you might be sleeping in yourself today, what time d'you get to bed?"

"Hmm, well actually I haven't been to bed yet, I'm just going to drop home for a quick shower and a shave and then I was wondering if you could give us a bit of a hand at the morgue. We'll need skilled people to accompany the relatives when they have to identify the . . . well you know when they come for . . ."

"Yes, yes I know. Should I go straight to the morgue?"

"Yes, that's right there's a consulate post there. You'll see the girls from the office, just wait for me there."

"Do you need me to bring anything David? Is there anything else they need there?"

"Well I don't think they've got much to work with, anything you think they might need would be great."

"Okey dokey, I'll see you there then."

The blanket of disillusion was starting to lift. Who said this was over? What had made me think that today would be normal or ordinary?

As I showered I made a mental list of all the things that I thought would be needed for the dead, their families and those who came to care for them. I had been to the Sanglah morgue only once before on the night of the fatal stabbing. I remembered it as a stark, grimy place with only a half a dozen fridges at the most. There were few luxuries in this section of the hospital, not even a sheet or a blanket. I remembered the night that I had delivered our unfortunate patient, there was another man lying stark naked on the mortuary slab, defrosting for the morning's autopsy session. When I asked the attendant for a sheet to cover his frozen client he declined to assist, claiming that he did not stock any linen in his department. The relatives of my patient came to grieve their tragic loss with 'the Ice-Man' in full view. I remember thinking that the mortuary assistant must have been almost as cold as his clients! He had the appearance of a Mr. Hyde character type with large rotten teeth, dark gnarly skin and a glass eye; it was as if he had been hand picked for the job! There were no niceties here, no bowl of lilies on the mahogany table, no soft lights and pictures of sunsets over the ocean embossed with inspiring words for the bereaved. This morgue I knew, was not much more than a butcher's slab.

I would have a light breakfast, as I suspected that my appetite would be less than sharp later in the day. As I sipped on coffee I jotted down a shopping list of supplies that I thought I might need: disinfectant, rubber boots, gloves, masks, fly spray, hand wash, tissues, tarpaulins, buckets, black marking pens and stick-on labels. I restocked my trusty waist bag, and checked my wallet for cash. My finances were sadly depleted, and I knew there was no money in the bank. I had not yet collected my wages from the Bali International School (B.I.S.) so I would stop there on the way to the hospital to get enough cash for the mortuary supplies.

Tony's thickset silhouette appeared at the door just as I was about to leave. He was smiling just like he usually did, and I felt a sense of relief. We had not communicated since Saturday night and if he could be this jovial, then surely he had not known anyone who had been injured or killed. We sat for another cup of coffee and Tony's smile quickly changed to a heavy brow as we spoke of the magnitude of the event. We spoke of the casualty figures, and the death toll with mutual disbelief.

Tony would drive for me today, he would be with me for as much as he could, but I knew that the morgue gates would be as close as he would go. He seemed concerned about my welfare or was it my ability to cope in such a place?

"You sure you're going to be okay in there? You sure you can handle this?"

"I'll be fine, I won't be alone you know and the dead are certainly not going to come after me!"

"It's not that Kim, you don't know, you don't know what's happening. I've been to the banjars (community halls). I've sat with the elders, they say this was a bomb, maybe even two or three bombs and nobody knows why. They say the men that did this are Al'Qaeda, fanatic Muslims. If this is true then you know what this could mean here don't you?"

Tony was suggesting that there could be an all-out religious war on the island. Bali's population was largely Hindu with strong Islamic sectors in various regions. While the relationship between the Hindus and the Muslims was usually one of mutual tolerance, it was tense in some regions. Surely not every Islamic person in Bali would have sanctioned such an atrocity, but this event could become a catalyst for a catastrophic blood bath.

Tony went on. "The elders, they see it, they know this is not ordinary people that have done this, but the young ones they don't! You know how it is, one start to fight, then all start to fight and you won't stop it! It could be bad Kim, it could be very dangerous here, this why I tell you take care, you be careful everywhere, and any problem you call me straight away you hear?"

I heard, and I knew that this was a very real possibility. I had seen the October riots during the presidential elections of 1999 when bands of men took to the streets in cars and trucks, cutting down trees, blocking major intersections and setting fire to everything they could. These gangs had disappeared as quickly as they had come after the ballots had been counted. No one knew who they were or from whence they came.

We left for the school and I was glad that Tony was accompanying me. It would be good to talk rather than be alone with my own thoughts. The school car park was almost empty; it was a forgone conclusion that the Bali International School would not be open for students today. Tony parked the car and opted to stay for a chat with the security guards while I went on into the school. Jorge Nelson the school's principal was in his office and greeted me warmly with his smooth American accent.

"Hey girl, I heard you've been busy! You know there's no school today, why don't you take some time out, take a break?"

"Wish I could Jorge, I'm off to the morgue today, just came by to pick up my wages so I can go get some supplies."

"Oh my Lord, what a thing, what a terrible thing this is. Well you know that we're all behind you here, whatever you need you just holler." Jorge called out to the finance manager and instructed her to issue my pay in cash immediately. I thanked him and as I turned to leave he spoke again. "Oh Kim, by the way there'll be a small gathering for Delores later this week, you're welcome to come, I'll mail you the details."

"Delores? Is someone leaving?" Delores was not a familiar name to me. I assumed that one of the teachers had been unnerved by the bombing and was making a hasty trip home.

"Oh Lord, you haven't heard? Delores Sansbury, our primary relief teacher, she was at the Sari Club, they identified her yesterday."

I was dumbstruck, I did not know Delores but this was too close to home, much too close. "Oh, I'm sorry. I'm so sorry. God this is awful Jorge, it's a bloody nightmare."

"That it is, Kim, that it certainly is and I know that you'll be busy, but I just ought to mention that we'll need some heavy duty first aid kits around here as well. Seems that this was directed specifically towards Westerners and we're sitting ducks here. I'm going to do my damnedest to make sure nothing ever happens, but just in case it ever does we'll need those kits!"

Entertaining the idea of a bomb on campus made me feel sick to the stomach, but Jorge was right, the threat was indeed very real.

"A scary thought Jorge, but I'll start working on it soon as I can. You give me a budget and I'll give you kits."

On the ride to the supermarket I could feel the weight of the day already resting heavy on my shoulders. Few words were spoken as we loaded Tony's Toyota hatchback with buckets full of the listed items that I had purchased at the store. As we approached the hospital I slipped on an old green surgical gown, pulled my hair in a tight ponytail and tied on a surgical mask. Tony was nervous and seemed almost repelled at the thought of why I was dressing this way. I gave Tony directions to the morgue's entrance and we could see from a distance that traffic was being redirected at the first turn. We had no trouble getting through the road block once Tony had explained our presence and gestured towards me sitting in the passenger seat dressed in my green medical garb. I could not believe what I saw as we turned the last bend that would lead us to the morgue's entrance. A wall of people, three to four deep, were clambering at the surrounding walls, standing one on top of the other to get a better view of the sights within. As we opened the car doors the stench of death and rotting flesh was more vile than words could describe. Tony was already looking pale and started to sweat profusely. He motioned to the guards who would assist me with my supplies, and asked once again if I thought I would be able to cope. I was starting to wonder the same thing myself, but I thought it best that I let Tony go quickly before he passed out at my feet!

Immediately inside the compound were two large refrigerated trucks parked back to back. To the left of the vehicles was the mortuary building itself, and to the right a small open marquee that was the consular post. I must admit to having felt rather over-dressed, as when I looked around me the volunteers that were there were not medics or off-duty military personnel, but surfers, students and housewives! The dress code it seemed was a singlet, shorts and a pair of beach sandals!

Approaching the marquee I could see several familiar faces. David was there of course, along with Angie, one of the consular assistants and Joan, a senior nurse from New Zealand whom I had worked with at the clinic. After dropping my bucket load of supplies I greeted them all with a smile and a nod and wondered what would be the most appropriate thing to say on a day like this? Something like "A hell of a disaster we're having!" . . . or "Stinking hot day!" maybe? But I decided that a simple "Good morning all," would suffice. Greetings returned, I noticed that David had half a smile on his face as he looked my way, and so I decided to make jest of myself before everyone else did!

"So, do I feel like the jolly green giant or what?"

"Oh no, not at all! You're probably the only one here appropriately dressed, Kim!" David's diplomacy was a gift. Joan however was a little more to the point.

"Looks bloody hot under all that lot if you ask me!" And it was!

The putrid stench that hung in the air was sickening and I decided to take advantage of some local mentholated oil (minyak angin) that I had packed in my waist bag. A few drops on my face-mask might help to ease the pungency of the odor. I offered the fragrant oil around to the small group at the table and all accepted except for Joan. She was from the old school and as tough as old leather boots, but she definitely had what it took to be here.

No other people had come to our table apart from a few Indonesian police, and an Anglican minister from the Australian Army. I was starting to wonder what I was doing there. Where were the relatives that we were supposed to assist? I broached David on the subject and it seemed that the Australian Federal Police and forensics teams had arrived, and had stopped relatives from doing direct identification at the morgue. Apparently there had been a body mix-up on one of the earlier releases and no more bodies would be allowed to go until further notice. As we ended our conversation two tall, dark, well dressed men approached. The older of the two spoke to David, and although he initially appeared to be calm and composed, it soon became apparent that 'calm and composed' he was not. He was speaking loudly and I could clearly hear every word as he addressed David.

"Look, it was there yesterday morning! I saw it! It was there, and last night it was gone! It was her ring, it was our wedding ring and I want it back!"

David was trying his best to placate this man, "Yes I know Sir but . . ."

"Look I saw her yesterday, I know she's in there, she's not burned up like all the rest of them, she's all in one piece, she's still my wife and I want to see her now!! I want her ring back!!"

At first I was taken aback by this man's concern over a simple band of gold when we were standing only meters away from the fleshy remnants and scorched corpses of so many, of so much lost love and life. How could he concern himself with such a thing? As I puzzled over his reaction it became clear that this was not just a trinket, not just a jewel, it was her. The ring was all that he could hold, all that was left of what they had once had. I imagined her a beauty, dark of skin and hair, and in the prime of her youth. They had probably only recently married, and could even have been on their honeymoon. The ring was all he had left and now that too was gone.

As I watched him pleading to see her again, I thought of the marriage vows. "What God has joined together let no man put asunder." What kind of man or men had committed this atrocity, under what pretense and in the name of what kind of God? What right did they think they had to rip so many, so young from the prime of their lives?

This desperate man's anger turned to uncontrollable sobs as he clutched at the arms of his male companion and buried his head on his shoulder as he almost collapsed with the grief that had overcome him.

I thought I would address David to see if I could help in any way, perhaps go into the morgue with the man to see if we could find her or the ring again, but it seemed that David had already considered this and thought wiser of it.

"It would be no use Kim. Yesterday the team in there did a great job. Had everyone labeled that was identified, separated the males from the females, and tried to put all the parts in some order but this morning when they came back, they had all been mixed up again, and unfortunately some of the jewelry has gone missing."

"You're kidding me aren't you? You mean people would be as low as to do that? Steal gold from the dead?"

"It seems that way. It's appalling to think that someone would even think of doing such a thing, even worse is that it's making the identification task even harder if these specific pieces of jewelry are missing." I thought of 'Mr. Hyde' the mortuary assistant. I could imagine him picking the gold out of people's teeth to supplement his meager wage. A position like his would probably pay only about 200,000 Rupiahs (approximately USD $20.00) a month at the most.

One could hardly blame him for trying to supplement his income in any way that he could.

I searched for some other reason that the ring may have gone missing and David listened to my theory. "Perhaps someone's filed the jewelry? Put it in envelopes or something once the body has been identified? I might find this man's wedding ring for him, at least I can give it a go."

"No harm in trying, Kim, there are a group of ladies working on the I.D. just over there." David gestured to the small reception area at the entrance to the mortuary building itself.

Inside the building I was once again astounded by the caliber of people that had come forward to do what most would not even imagined themselves capable of, not even in their wildest dreams. A small group of women, housewives, teachers and artists were working intensely over reams of paper; lists of the missing, lists of the dead, lists of the families. Many of the women were from the B.I.W.A. (Bali International Woman's Association), a group who regularly meet for lunch, charity events or art classes, but today they were here, and instead of piecing together brightly colored scraps of fabric to make a brilliantly colored blanket, they were patching together a quilt of lost lives, tainted and stained with the blood of the innocent.

"Good morning ladies. I was wondering if anyone knows anything about what's happening with the valuables that are found on the bodies?"

"Huh! So were we!" A young blonde woman so aptly replied.

"Well I have some guy who's pretty upset about his wife's ring that's gone missing. Is anyone filing this stuff or putting it away?" I enquired.

"Well someone is but it's not us! A couple of things seem to have gone missing overnight. Bloody sick if you ask me! We had all this lot sorted yesterday," she gestured towards the innermost rooms and vacant lot behind the morgue that was now lined with orange plastic covered corpses, "and now it's just a big bloody mess again."

Several women wearing t-shirts from the Buddhist Woman's Association were laying small posies of flowers at the head of each body. Any sweet perfume that these blooms struggled to emit was quickly drowned in the overwhelming stench. Teams of volunteer youths wearing Red Cross t-shirts carted bodies and shoveled ice that melted almost as quickly as it was placed. I wondered at this group of youngsters, boys and girls that looked to be no more than teenagers. How diligently they worked, silently without complaint they trudged through their unthinkable duties, without so much as a shriek or a squeal, most did not even cover their nose or make any gesture of distaste. They just worked on and on, young guardians of the dead. Many of those that they lifted and carried would be the same age as themselves. How did these youngsters cope? How would their young minds overcome the images of horrors unthinkable that would be branded into their thoughts for ever? How should they take comfort when they woke in the night with fears and ghosts that tugged at their sanity? This wasn't fair, this just was not fair, and yet here they all were, here we all were in a quagmire of death and decay.

The young blonde lady broke my thoughts and I was glad for I did not want to stay around these parts for any longer than I really had to.

"We've had terrible problems labeling this lot. Even when we get an I.D. we can't get anything to stick. The tie on labels slip off, the stick on labels won't stick, it's a bloody nightmare. We're running around in circles doing the same stuff all over again."

"Have you tried writing on the bodies with a parcel marker?" I knew what I had said was stupid as soon as I had said it and the woman almost told me as much.

"What skin????"

Few of the bodies had enough skin that was not burned or scorched to such an extent that it would be able to lend its gruesome canvas to names or numbers.

"Yes, sorry that was really stupid of me! I've heard that proper body bags are on their way, I'll see if I can chase them up for you a bit later. Well . . . thanks for you help anyway, I'll go tell this man that I can't' find his wife or the ring then."

"Look, if I'm not wrong she's in there." The blonde woman gestured towards the two cold storage trucks whose engines droned as they struggled to cool their gruesome load. "But you'll have a hell of a job finding her, there's about a hundred others in there with her, and most have all lost their labels."

I thought better of any attempt to retrieve the mans gold ring from either of the trucks and as I wondered back to the consular post I could see that the man who had lost his wife had gone. As I walked I found my thoughts drifting again. What if one of mine were lost, missing, or had not come home on that night? What if I had been told that my son or daughter was dead in the back of truck? I would surely go insane, become wild, a she-wolf ripping and tearing with tooth and claw at every makeshift blood-soaked shroud until I found my own, until I could embrace them, see them, take them to a place where I would wash and clothe them for one last time. I would want to hold the lifeless cold hand of all that I had loved, to farewell and to lay to rest. What torture to lose and not to see what you have lost? Not to be able to give it substance or be able to embrace and then to let it go?

10
The List of Heads

The midday sun was merciless as it shone down, lending it's warmth to the macabre recipe for decomposing flesh. The wall of ghoulish sight seekers strained to get a better view over the mortuary fence, and it appeared some action was about to take place on the trucks. The stench of death was overwhelming as the truck doors swung open and several volunteers, men and women, dressed in the standard 'shorts and T-shirt' garb started to climb inside . . .

This morning's team of helpers looked as if they would be more at home on the Kuta shore break than here amongst all this. The blonde, bearded, tanned and carefree type, that were about to exchange the rolling surf of 'Dreamland' for the repugnant slush of 'Deadman's Land.' The task at hand was to remove the makeshift shrouds from the bodies, try to re-label them and then place the corpses or parts thereof into one of the new body bags, a few of which had already arrived. The freshly wrapped corpses would then have to be moved from the first truck into the second, which was empty and considerably colder. I could not believe how this team worked with what seemed like a complete lack of concern for 'self'. They worked with bare hands and feet, skin to skin with the decaying dead. I offered rubber boots, gloves and masks only to be declined and almost shunned as I had disturbed the process, interrupted their system which I suspected was one of extreme focus to the point that they would not break thought for anything that might remind them of where they really were and what they were really doing. They toiled without falter, lifting and carting parcels of every size, traipsing through the bloody slush that oozed from the pile. I sincerely hoped that these servants of the dead would not slip or fall into the gruesome quagmire as they strained to lift the larger bodies. Some bags looked enormous, and I thought of the rugby coach that I had seen on the previous day in the wards. These big bags were probably his boys, the boys that he could not find.

As the odor settled so did the flies. It was time to reach into my buckets of supplies and wage a one-man war on these persistent pests that had descended en masse. Armed with my single can of fly spray I aimed at the buzzing black dots and one or two even seemed to fall into a death dive, but for every one conquered a dozen more were waiting to launch their assault. Feeling about as useless as mammary glands on a Hereford stud I decided to take up my post at the Consular tent once again. A young woman was engaged in conversation with David and was obviously here on an assignment rather than for any other purpose. She appeared to be barely in her twenties, tall and athletic with broad shoulders and well defined facial features. She was fair of skin and wore no make-up or jewelry that was apparent excepting a heavy diver's wrist watch. Her hair was pulled back into a short blonde ponytail at the nape of her neck, her t-shirt and dungarees were navy blue, and she wore heavy standard issue black leather boots. My initial guess was that she was with the Federal Police, and after a short conversation with David my assumption was confirmed. 'Jill', as David had introduced, was with the A.F.P. We shook hands and David excused himself to accept another phone call so I decided to make light conversation with the police woman as she was obviously alone, although did not seem at all out of sorts on her solitary mission.

"So, it's a pity that it has been something like this that brings you to our island, have you been to Bali before or is this your first time?"

"No, never been, it's not my type of place really." Jill was straight to the point as she gazed off in the direction of the trucks and the activity within.

"Yes, funny really isn't it, you either love this place or you just don't. I see a lot of people come through here and they either hate it and never come back, or they love it and never leave!"

"Hmmm. I suppose you do." This conversation was going to be really hard work as my attempts at small talk hardly managed to gain any response at all from the young police woman. I decided to attempt a more intelligent approach to see if I could stimulate more of a reaction.

"So, I hear that the relatives of the deceased are no longer doing a direct I.D. here at the morgue?" I enquired.

"That's correct. They should never have been allowed in here in the first place." Jill did not break her gaze and was giving nothing away.

"Yes, it must be awful for those people having to come here to find someone and see all this. It's been a bit of a mess as I understand; not enough fridges and cold storage, no labels, no body bags. The volunteers in there have really had an uphill battle trying to keep on top of it all."

"Yes I'm sure they have, but we can't have any more relatives coming through here. Our people are not culturally conditioned to these situations; Australians are not used to viewing their dead like this."

I was completely dumbstruck by her statement so I decided to go for some sort of clarification on her comment, which I thought was, to say the least, a little bizarre.

"I'm sorry?"

"This is not culturally acceptable to us. It's best that our people are kept away from this."

Jill's answer was once again brief and to the point, although it still didn't seem to make a hell of a lot of sense to me and so I decided to challenge her.

"And you're trying to tell me that there is a culture that finds this sort of thing acceptable??"

Jill did not respond and excused herself as she headed back into the hospital grounds.

Turning back to face the rest of the party at the table I noticed that boxes of food and refreshments had been delivered and I wondered how anyone could even consider eating in a place like this. The local police however did not seem to have a problem with the surrounds and helped themselves to small packets of rice, drinking water and cups of coffee. The smell of the clove-cured cigarettes as they finished their meal was a welcome reprise from other less-than-sweet odors close by.

The last of the bodies from the first truck had now been repackaged and relocated into the second truck. As they sealed the doors on the loaded refrigerated container I could not help wondering where the trucks had come from and what their regular cargo would be. I decided to share my thoughts with Joan as she stood close by.

"Where do you think these trucks came from then Joan?"

"Don't know Kim, don't think I know."

"Me neither, but remind me never to buy ice-cream again will you!"

As we gazed and pondered the logistics of storing and preserving over two hundred rotting corpses, I was shocked yet again at the next event that we were about to witness. A large water hose was hauled into the back of the empty truck and the bloody rancid slush that had oozed from the grizzly cargo was hosed down and swept out to the car park where we stood. A river of dark brown stinking liquid flowed across the ground, around our feet and onto the grassed area behind us that led to the hospital wards. I was silently glad for having worn my old sneakers again as even though they had seen better days, the soles still had good tread and were intact. I thought how the policewoman's boots would have been an even better option, although I still felt that I had a distinct advantage when I looked around to see the less fortunate ones in open toe sandals!

Watching this morbid river of death flow farther into the hospital grounds I decided that the large packs of pine antiseptic might at least serve as some guard against the disease that would surely breed here if this effluent were left untreated. I opened the first of the large four liter containers and started dowsing down the puddles over the asphalt and onto the grass. I could not help but notice that all eyes were upon me and I decided that a little humor might break the heaviness that hung in the air. Turning toward the consulate post I held the container to the fore and in my best television voice played to the audience.

"The next time YOU have a disaster use Pine O' Clean. Tough on germs, gentle on your feet!"

My antics raised a few eyebrows and a few smiles and David shook his head as he did so. "Oh Kim, you're forever the clown!"

"Not really, I suppose I shouldn't have done that, but you know David, if we didn't laugh, we'd all be . . . well you know . . ." my silly antics were back-firing as my voice faltered. ". . . we'd all be . . ."

David finished my sentence for me. "Yes I know, Kim, a little bit of black humor won't hurt, if we didn't laugh a little bit we'd all be in tears!"

"I was thinking something like we'd all go stark raving bloody mad actually!" I replied.

I poured the rest of the solution behind the back wheels of the truck and as I did so more of the stinking fluid from within was splashed out with the last sweeping motions of the volunteers inside. I felt the droplets of tepid wetness settle on my cheek and on the back of my neck and shoulder, baptized by the essence of death itself.

When I finished my task I returned to the marquee and washed my face three times over with the bottled drinking water on hand. The staff that remained at the consular table looked bemused by my actions, not having seen the incident that prompted my dowsing.

"What happened to you, you feeling hot or what?" asked Angie the consular assistant.

"Don't ask." I replied "You really don't want to know! I just hope I don't get lucky this afternoon 'cos I sure as hell won't get to kiss anybody smelling like this!"

Feeling mildly refreshed, I looked up to see one of the volunteer surfers making toward me, a young man who typified the sport that he represented. Light sandy hair, tanned, with a light muscular physique and as he spoke his Californian accent was the perfect match of his physical being.

"Ah, you look like a girl that knows what she's about. Allow me to introduce myself, Jeff's my name."

"Pleased to meet you Jeff, I'm Kim, what can I do for you?" I was hoping that Jeff could not smell my less than aromatic perfume as we chatted, but it seemed that his sense of smell had also been numbed by the constant foulness that was in the air.

"Well I need this list taken up to the I.D. room in the main hospital building. You know where it is don't you?"

I remembered seeing the room in question on the upper level of the E.R. building on the previous day. "Yes sure, what do you need there?"

Jeff presented a folded piece of paper and went on to explain my mission. "I need you to take this list of heads to the ladies that are working on this up there."

"Sorry?" Jeff's simple request had not quite registered as I tried to fathom this 'list of heads'. Were they 'Heads' of departments?, 'Heads' of families?, or volunteers that were 'heading' certain tasks?

Jeff unfolded the paper and as he spoke the horrific implication of my mission became apparent.

"This list here, the list of heads, Bubba says there are about a dozen listed so far, but there'll probably be more later."

'THE LIST OF HEADS' was exactly that. A hand-written description of all decapitated human heads that had been detailed so far. I had no desire to read the list but as I glanced at the document in my hand I could see that the list looked to be double the number that Jeff had quoted.

I took the paper and I could not help but think of the grim tidings that this hand written note would bring to those waiting for news, looking for their own and yet hoping not to find them, at least not here, not on this list. I headed for the main hospital building through the grassed area behind the morgue that was now a storage place for hundreds of plywood coffins that were stacked one on top of the other and three or four rows deep. The coffins were empty and would not be occupied until one by one each body had been identified and released. As I walked, another woman headed in the same direction walked along side of me. She was a tall mature European woman and she spoke with a heavy accent. Her long blonde hair was plaited in two braids, she wore an apron and boots and I couldn't help thinking that she looked as if she should be working on a dairy farm rather than where I knew she had been. She stared straight ahead as she spoke.

"This is so much a shocking thing, what I see here . . . all that I 'ave seen. All those boys . . . all those poor young boys! They 'ave not lived, they 'ave seen nothing, still so young. They meant no one harm, they just wanted to enjoy themselves and why this?! They did not deserve this! I 'ave not seen anything like this not even when I was in Timor."

I guessed by her statement that she was experienced at this sort of thing, with a disaster relief organization or perhaps forensics.

"So you've worked in this field before? Seen a lot of this sort of thing then?" I asked as I struggled to keep up the pace.

"No, no! Good heavens no, I just happened to be there in times of trouble. But this, Aaaahhhhh, this is the worst, never 'ave I seen this so bad like this. Those boys, so many, so young. They 'ave done nothing, why must they die like this . . ."

The woman was almost ranting and I realized that expressing her feelings the way that she did might be only thing that was keeping her sane, so I listened as she continued on saying the same thing over and over again.

The paper that I carried seemed to almost turn my fingers cold as I thought of the tragic data that it bore. I climbed the stairs to the relatives' I.D. room and was more than glad to hand over the document to a woman who seemed to be expecting the delivery.

As I walked back to the morgue through the hospital grounds the shadows had become longer and the sun was sinking down behind the taller buildings. Across the courtyard and heading toward me I could see a Hindu holy man with a small entourage of lay priests as well as a few women dressed in traditional garb that had carried the baskets of offerings for the hospital's temple. As the small band approached I could see that the head priest was Tony's father. He walked a few paces ahead of the group, dressed all in white — a sarong, sash, and shirt — with his thinning silver hair pulled into a tight top-not and decorated with a small red flower. He carried the traditional wooden staff that he swung before him as he paced slowly but purposefully down the pathway. While he was part of the group I could not help thinking that he looked alone in his thoughts, separate from those that chattered behind him. His bearded face expressed both concern and indifference and I wondered what he saw here today? I wondered if he saw what I did, the bloody slaughterhouse and human waste or whether with his gifted vision he saw the lost souls walking — for as a 'Serimpu' (the highest level of common caste priest) he would surely have the ability to do so. According to Balinese belief, the spirits of the dead walk among us until such time as the correct rites of passage have been performed, allowing the soul to pass on. It is assumed that those who die in tragic circumstances and before their time will have problems moving on as many would not even realize that they were dead.

The spiritual beliefs of the Balinese culture are strong. This was not a set of 'ghost stories', shared between the superstitious few, but a fact of life, a firm belief of commoners and high society alike. Even politicians and scholars had no doubt that the 'walking dead' were just as much a part of life as the living. If this were so, then surely these hospital grounds would be buzzing with souls wondering what on earth they were doing in this place rather than soaking up the sun on Kuta beach! As communicators for the dead, it would be the job of the Balinese priests and shamans to placate and calm the spirits with specific mantra and ceremonies, many of which had already been performed and would culminate in a massive 'resting of souls' gathering in weeks to come.

The small party of priests was getting closer and I thought better of greeting Tony's father on this day. He would not recognize me, and I as a caretaker of the dead in their physical form would be 'unclean', and it would be less than polite to address a holy man in this state. I turned the last corner to the morgue as the pious group disappeared into the hospital's car park.

As I trod through the putrid quagmire leading to the back entrance of the morgue I was reminded of my less-than-holy tasks for the day.

The stinking river that had flowed from the trucks had turned the grassed area behind the morgue into a muddy mess, and all and sundry were passing through it, most without closed in shoes or foot wear. I wondered if they realized what had caused this marsh under foot, and if they would still be as game to come sightseeing if they did.

Towards the gates leading to the consular post I saw another familiar face. Made (pronounced Maday) Dani was a surfer from Sanur beach, and many was the time we caught an afternoon southerly breeze together on the sail boards out over the reef. Made was a man now, although back in my days of sun and surf he was just a boy whose knees and elbows were regularly patched up by yours truly. I liked Made for the mischief that he was. He had the hide to stand up for what he thought was right despite the peer pressure from his own kind. For all his antics he was down to earth and honest and I had never seen him lie or cheat. Made had always been muscular and well built and as a man he was even more so, he was handsome in a rugged sort of way, and he flashed a broad smile as I caught his eye on my approach.

"Mbok Kim!" ('Mbok' pronounced 'Mok' was a polite way to address a sister or female more senior than yourself). "What are you doing here?"

"Well I could ask you the same question Made!"

"I'm here for Lidia. You know her? I'm sure you know her! She live same street as you before in Bumi Ayu. She come to see you play when you sing with the band in Sanur, she always come when you sing!"

"Oh I can't remember Made, I meet so many people. Is she here? Did she lose someone?"

"Oh no! She die! She's going to Sari Club, and now she dead. She still look okay though, for sure we know that it's her. She daughter still young, she come for the body, so I help for that. Are you sure you not remember her? I'm sure you do."

Made pulled out a photograph of a middle aged blonde woman sitting at a restaurant laughing with some friends. I recognized her and recalled having several conversations with her at the restaurant where the band had played.

"Yes, now I remember, I'm so sorry Made, is her daughter okay?"

"Okay but not really okay, still very sad, but she happy 'cos she said her Mum still smile even when dead! At least she can see her Mum. I been in there . . ." Made motioned towards the mortuary building. "I see many in there you not know who they are! Just look like 'babi guling'! (roast pig). They bastard that do this Kim! They really big bastard!"

"That's for sure Made. Well I'm sorry about Lidia, I'd better go, you take care now."

"You too Mbok Kim, you look after your boys good, Bali not like before now, not at all."

Made was right. This was one hell of a wake-up call for our sleepy island. Lidia's death was another tragedy that was too close to home for me. I wondered who else would not be here tomorrow once the dust had settled and cleared. While I had few truly close friends, I knew a lot of people. Who would not be there tomorrow in the supermarket, at the school, at the ladies' lunches or which of the musicians would not show up for band practice or for next Saturday night's performance? Who of my health insurance clients would not renew next year's policy, and would any of my regular patients not come back to see me ever again? Would any of my prenatal ladies have lost their husbands, or babies that came for checks have lost their parents? It would take weeks if not months to take stock of all those that had been lost as result of this atrocious act.

11
Who's Lucky and Who's Not?

All conversation seemed to have run dry at the consular post and my thoughts once again turned inwards as I pondered the reality of what had happened and the outcome of what could have been. What if I had been there? What if it was me in the back of one of the trucks or laid out in pieces for someone to put back together like some macabre jigsaw puzzle for my family to identify? I would never want my people to have to go through this, to have to look for me in this sort of mess. I looked at the rings on my fingers. My jewelry was unique, not the sort of thing that you would find in Goldmart, but then again fingers and arms would easily become detached in a blast of this size. Perhaps I should get a tattoo? But what part of the body would I put such a branding, the torso, the head? What if I was burned and all identifying flesh marks would be lost? Was it time for us all to get indestructible miniature canisters containing personal I.D. data to wear around our necks? No . . . trinkets like these could still come adrift; perhaps such a pellet or microchip could be implanted under the skin or in a tooth? I realized that my thoughts were becoming somewhat irrational, like something out of a far-fetched sci-fi drama. Perhaps it was the lack of sleep or just the effect of being thrown into a situation that was almost surreal.

I tried to clear my thoughts and go into reality mode, but I was stuck in morbid introspection. As I stood and contemplated I redefined my perception of luck. Were you lucky to die quickly and with little suffering, or were you lucky to survive burned with searing pain only to succumb to death's cloak in the end? Were you lucky to die whole, in one piece and unmarked, or were you lucky to be instantly vaporized saving relatives the pain of seeing your roasted mutilated corpse?

There seemed to be little else for me to do in the wards of the dead, so I decided to take my leave. Joan and most of the consular staff had left, so I fare-welled those few that remained and made my way back to the hospital car park where I would find a taxi. One cab had just dropped several tourists at the emergency entrance so there was no need to wait. It was a relief to ease back into the rear seat of the car, and I hoped that the driver could not detect the odor of my clothes and footwear, for my own sense of smell had been temporarily numbed by the intense aromas that I had experienced throughout the day.

It was almost sunset now and my house was unoccupied apart from the maid who was just bringing in the washing from the yard. I was hesitant to enter my home in what I felt was a stinking shroud of death, and so I went only as far as the laundry where I disrobed and threw all that I had worn including my shoes, into a bucket. I wrapped myself in an old sarong and instructed Ketut to burn all the things that I had discarded immediately. I could see by the look on her face and that she was already contemplating resurrecting the items that she thought could be salvaged, as most things still had some wear left in them. I decided to make absolutely sure that she knew why these things had to be burned.

"Ketut, I want you to burn all of this NOW, these clothes are soaked in 'sari mayat'! (The essence of corpses)."

Any thoughts she had of recycling my clothes were immediately banished!

When I showered I must have scrubbed myself ten times over and washed my hair at least three times. Dried and dressed I allowed myself a few moments reprieve before I left to collect my sons from their father's house about ten minutes drive away. The phone rang and it was my parents calling from Adelaide, naturally they had been concerned. I knew exactly what they were going to say, and my Mother spoke first.

"Hello my love . . . oh my dear, what a terrible thing this is. How are you holding up? Are you and the boys okay?"

"We're fine Mum, we'll be just fine. I'm on my way to get the boys now . . . they've been at their father's, I've been a bit busy you know."

"I imagine that you have, we've seen it all on the news. They don't even know how many are dead yet do they?"

"No Mum, I don't think they will for a while. Even some that are still alive now may not make it in the end and they'll never be able to count the ones that will never be missed, the prostitutes and the beggars, no one will even know they're gone."

"Good lord, all those poor people, and most of them so young. Well, you know you can always come home, we'll pay for your tickets and all, and you know there's plenty of room here."

"I know Mum, there's just too much to do right now, much too much. Anyway I hear that you have a sniper down there! I could get shot walking the dog if I come home!" I had heard on the news about the 'copy cat' sniper that had already targeted and killed several people in the Adelaide city streets.

"Yes, well that's a bit different, it's not like we have terrorists blowing people up everywhere!" My Mother replied.

"End result's still the same Mum! You still end up dead. I guess we just have to hope our number's still a long way off!"

My Father took the phone and in his brash north-country British accent laid it on the line! "You should bloody well come home you should lassie! Ya' Mum wants you 'ome, so does that girl of yours!" Dad knew that this would tug at my conscience, bomb or no bomb!

"I know Dad, let's just see shall we, let's just see for now."

The last of the sun's rays disappeared over the paddies as I left to collect my two boys from their father's house. The old sedan was obliging and I decided to stop at Elena's house on the way. Their property was right on the beach and it was always a pleasure to visit. I was greeted by Elena's husband, Tom, who as usual had a beer in one hand and a cigarette in the other. Tom was a real character, a salty-dog, laid back, and he spoke with a deep slow drawl. Born in Japan and raised in California he had a physical presence that denied his years and his habits! You just couldn't help but like Tom.

"Hey there Kimmy, you look a little weary. Come on in and have yourself a beer!" This was Tom's standard greeting even though I had never drunk a glass of beer in my life!

"Pass! Haven't got a vodka and lime have you?"

"No, no I don't think I do, but I can give you a glass o' wine. Come on over here and have a seat, Elena's just finishing up in the shower." Tom poured a glass of red while he continued to speak. "So what d'you think about all this then Kim? What a thing? Jesus Christ who would 'a thought here eh? Bastards!"

Elena appeared from the house and Tom poured another glass. We sat in the outdoor living area, which was a common feature in houses on this island. There was little need to protect yourself from the elements, and there was no sense in building walls that would block the welcome sea breeze on balmy tropical nights. We sipped on wine and smoked clove cigarettes as we talked, I was horrified to hear of how close Elena's two older boys had come to being injured or even killed in the bombing.

"You know it's weird," She said in her Swiss Italian accent. "Most of the high school kids were going to Paddy's that night, but they all seemed to get held up by different things. One group of boys got held up because the taxi was late, another lot because one boy forgot his wallet and had to come back for it and the girls were running late because one of them had stomach cramps so they were waiting to see if she would feel better."

"Good Lord I didn't know that! My God I hate to imagine . . . shit, it's not worth thinking about!" But I was thinking about it, and it made my blood run cold.

What if the bombers had been targeting these children? It was not beyond the realms of possibility that they had meant to catch these high school teenagers in the slaughter. The people that had claimed responsibility for this were not backward. They were a highly organized group with intelligence, facilities, finance and were trained in terrorist tactics. The Jemiah Islamyah (J.I.) was a radical, fanatic Islamic organization that was targeting Indonesia to become an exclusively Islamic state. So dedicated were they to their cause that sacrificing their own lives (suicide attacks) was considered heroism, a holy martyr's death. The main enemies of this faction were Americans and Jews. Why then had they chosen downtown Kuta as their target? Perhaps one reason would have been that Bali was indeed the only Hindu majority province left in the archipelago; by launching an attack such as this they could incite a religious war with intent of wiping out as many Hindus as they could.

The Sari Club would have been chosen as it denied free access to Indonesian Nationals, but why did they do this knowing that the majority of victims would be Australians? Why had they not waited for an American navy vessel to be in port when the night clubs of Kuta would be full of young American servicemen? Why had they chosen 11.15 pm to detonate the bomb? It was common knowledge that the nightlife in this area peaked at between mid-night and two a.m. If the bomb had exploded just an hour later they would have doubled the casualty count. It just did not make sense. Perhaps they really had targeted the expatriate teenage community that regularly attended Paddy's bar on a Saturday night. Many were American, or of American descent, and some indeed were Jewish. If this group of adolescents had been killed not one expatriate family on the Island would have been untouched; surely most would leave the Island which is exactly what the J.I. would have wanted.

We pondered these thoughts over the last dregs of wine and Elena spoke as I prepared to leave. "Well I don't know, I'm not superstitious but I can't help thinking that there was something looking out for those kids on Saturday night."

"Yeh, makes you think! Maybe angels really do watch over!"

"Well I hope so! Teo's still pretty shaken by it all though, he came pretty close you know, he said some guy's head landed right by his feet!"

Teo was Elena's oldest son. At twenty years old he was the sensitive type, a really nice kid, I could not imagine the horror that this would imprint on his young mind for the rest of his life.

"Shit! He must have been really close!"

"Yeh, pretty close! So many of them were, it's just a miracle that they're all still here! You know about the two girls in the taxi don't you? They're from your son's school, Nina and Dewi?"

"No . . . what happened?"

"The taxi they were in was really close, lifted up in the air when the bomb went off and the driver was killed instantly . . ."

"And!?"

"And they're okay, not even a scratch!"

"Shit! That has to be a miracle! I had no idea! I hope someone's talking to them about this, counselling I mean. This stuff could really mess them up especially at their age!"

"Yes I think so, Nina's going back to the States with her family, but Dewi of course will still be here. I think her parents are pretty switched on though. I'm sure they'll do something."

"Let's hope so, maybe I can talk to the school about organizing some groups or sessions with the kids that were there." I was the school nurse assigned to the Bali International School, but I could always make suggestions to the other international schools as the educators here were a pretty tight knit group and often shared ideas or facilities.

Elena continued to speak. "Yes but even worse is Armando. He was there and his parents didn't even know, and they still don't! He told them he was sleeping at a friend's place and went to Paddy's instead! A lot of kids got caught out on that night, the two girls in the taxi weren't supposed to be there either!"

"What!? You mean Armando's got to walk around with all this stuff in his head and he can't even tell his parents? It'll send him crazy! It'll fester in his brain!"

"Yeh I know, but I think he's talking to the student counselor about it for what it's worth, but I still think someone will have to sit him down with his parents and work this out."

"I hope so!" We were already standing at my car by this stage and I farewelled Elena, promising to keep in touch.

My ex-husband's family compound was only a short drive away, and I could not help noticing how quiet things were; even the streets of the Semawang red light district did not seem to be as lively as they usually were. The bars and cafes sported very few young 'night butterflies' in tight pants or short skirts, and over painted lips. Near to my husband's house the up-market 'tourist' restaurants that lined the main Sanur esplanade were empty, not a tourist in sight. Those holidaymakers that had not already left the island had chosen to stay within the safety of the confines of their hotels. The waitresses and waiters sat on walls and footpaths outside the eateries waiting patiently to welcome nobody at all.

My boys were quiet in the car, tired I guessed, as they liked to stay up to watch movies if there was no school. Kris was the first to speak being the more forthright of my two sons, and I was disturbed by what he had to say.

"Were you there Mummy? Were you at where the bomb was?"

"No my love, I was working at the hospital helping the people that were hurt, why?"

"We saw it all! All these black people lying all over the ground dead! It was really yukky and . . . "

Ben my eldest son interrupted. ". . . yeah and there was some guy without a head, and all these arms and legs everywhere . . ."

I could not believe what I was hearing. "What!? Where on earth did you see that!?"

"On the news, we saw EVERYTHING!"

Damn it! What point was there in trying to protect young ones from all this when modern technology brought it right into your home at prime viewing time? After all that I had not told them, they had actually seen more graphic and gory sights than I had! I decided to change the subject and enquired as to any dinner plans these two might have.

"So where do you guys want to eat?"

"McDonalds!" This was Kris's standard answer, as cheeseburgers were his all time favorite food.

"Well what about something healthy for a change, guys?"

Ben replied and although he was not so keen on burgers, even he was ready for a dose of junk food. "Are you kidding Mum? We've been living on rice and vegetables since yesterday. You know what Bapak's like! Beans, beans and more beans!"

"Okay, okay. But we'll get take-away from the drive-through, I don't want to sit in the restaurant okay?"

"But why?"

"It's American."

"And?"

"I'll tell you later when I'm not so tired!"

Shortly after we entered the house Kris requested a hug as he often did. Standing on the verandah we hugged each other tightly and even Ben joined in for a 'group hug', which was quite a surprise, as hugging your mother and your kid brother is pretty un-cool when you are thirteen!

As I embraced my two boys I held them with more purpose than I had ever done. Swaying gently I stroked Bens hair and nuzzled Kris's cheek as I thought of how lucky I was to be here, to be holding my children in my arms, I felt tears well up as I thought of the hundred or so other Mothers that had been robbed of this privilege, who would ache to hold their sons and daughters again, and never would.

Kris broke my thoughts. "Mummy, are you crying?"

"No . . . of course not! Come on let's have dinner. Your burgers are getting cold."

12
Hellfire and Brimstone
Tuesday October 15th

I was just finishing my coffee and contemplating my day when Tony appeared at the front door. He was smiling, which was a good sign, although he still seemed a little reserved, as if he had something on his mind.

I poured another coffee and questioned his thoughts.

"What's up Tony? Everything okay?"

"Yes okay but bit problem still. Nearly big fight in Denpasar last night. Could still be problem here. My father talk to me and say that he going to pray together with all Hindu priest and Moslem priest, Christian priest and Buddha one too. He say they try to stop big problem here. Could still be big problem you know Kim. You know what people are like here. You know some Hindu and Moslem they never like each other and now the Jihad do this it become much worse!"

I knew all too well of the rift between the two religions that was basically divided between the Javanese (Moslem) and the Balinese (Hindu). Although the two appeared to live in harmony, it was a very thin charade for some in a feud that went back as far as the 17th century. Each would blame the other for the petty crime, prostitution or uncouth behavior, but the truth be known they were as bad as or as good as each other. It was the individual that committed the crime, not the religion or the ethnicity.

Regardless of who was wrong or right or who threw the first stone, we were in a very volatile situation that could claim a hundred times the lives that had already been taken by the bomb itself. Community and religious leaders would be working overtime to get their message across to the masses, and all we could do was pray that it would work.

"You know Kim, it's really lucky about this Haji guy that do the rescue. He's going with many friends after the bomb. They rescue many people and he and his friend all Moslem. Now people hear this story and they think . . . this guy really good, like a hero now and he Muslim! This make people not fight, this really lucky thing."

"Really? I haven't heard about this, tell me more."

"His name Haji Bambang, he live in Kuta many years and he become head of Islamic youth group there, that's how he get so many boys to help him. He really good man this guy. He can stop for fighting here, you wait and see."

It was a strange irony that this man dedicated to a religion that had been touted by the very perpetrators of this atrocity, had done so much good. What damage these dogs of war had done, what a rift they had created. You could hardly blame a family for becoming bitter towards Islam when their children had been lost to a cruel and savage band that claimed this religion as their own. The truth be known, no religion, or sane leader, would have sanctioned this.

I had often contemplated the purpose of religion, when history has borne witness to countless atrocities in its name. Born and raised a Christian, and having lived in close quarters with both Islam and Hindu, I could see no point at all in slitting someone's throat over their chosen path. My ideals were perchance too simplistic, but perhaps this would be a better place if the world were full of simpletons like myself! I had now become a firm fence-sitter, refusing to be classified or grouped and I had often imagined Jesus, Buddha, Mother Mary, Mohammed, Abraham and the Hindu Dewas sitting around a large oak wooden table sipping tea, smiling and shaking their heads as they gazed down on us with dire pity. The conversation would be something like:

"I think we've thrown them a real wobbly with this religion thing don't you? Several millenniums and they still haven't figured it out!"

"Well they're only human I suppose!"

"Yes you're right! I think we'll be sitting here for eons before this lot gets it straight. I must admit I didn't think it would take them this long! The Catholics and the Christians are even fighting over the same book for Heavens sake!"

"Hear, hear! Anyone for another cup of tea, we may as well, there's no point in going thirsty. Looks like the Middle East is firing up again and someone just threw a grenade on the West bank!"

"Amen!"

While Tony checked my car and made sure that she would have enough oil to get me through the day, I opened my e-mail that I had not checked since Saturday morning. Most people had been considerate and sent very brief and concerned notes enquiring about our safety and wishing us well. I replied with an even briefer note that I sent to everyone in my address book.

There was one e-mail from an unfamiliar source and when I opened it I realized that it was from one of the Catholic nursing sisters from the Philippines, a woman that I had met at the International School Nurses Conference in Jakarta earlier in the year. What she had written to me was a blatant reminder of how narrow minded a religion could be. She wrote:

"Dear Kim,

I do hope this letter finds you well. We are all praying for you here and I am compelled to write to you with this message as I think it is something that you really need to know. I am sure you are the kind of person that realizes that in all bad there is some good. For all things there is a reason, and the reason for what has happened there is you! This is indeed divine intervention to show you the path to righteousness, a wonderful sign that you must repent, give up your sinful ways and come to Jesus.

Just think of all those poor souls that have been lost, those that will never find God because it is too late. What if it had been you there on that night Kim? Would you be saved or would you burn in hell with all the sinners? Would you be taken into Christ's arms or would you be consumed into hells eternity of suffering? Think about this Kim. This is a sign for YOU, nobody else but YOU. Cast your sins aside, give them up to Jesus and repent. Change your shameful ways and see the light that is waiting for you . . . etc etc" (This message was indeed four pages long!).

I wondered if it was worth replying to this, but there was something that this Nun needed to know, and so I wrote, "Thank you for your concerns, however you are not qualified to write this, you have not seen hell . . . I on the other hand have just spent two days there!"

Tony informed me that my car had consumed yet another gallon of oil and that she had been topped up and was once again roadworthy so it was time to go back in to Sanglah. I had printed two signs for my car with a red cross and 'VOLUNTEER MEDIC' written beneath. This would ensure that I would be able to gain admission to the Sanglah grounds as security had started to get a little tighter with the hoards of non-essential visitors that were passing through. I couldn't help thinking that the old car looked like a prop on a M.A.S.H. set, as her duco was indeed army green and she was still filthy dirty.

The Sanglah grounds had also started to look like something out of a military movie with two large khaki marquees that had been erected on the vacant grassed area outside of the emergency room. I decided that the best place to start today would be at the communications and counseling center that had been set up on the second floor of the E.R. block, but this area was already overcrowded with volunteers and helpers from every walk. Perhaps I would be better off to go directly to the wards and see what needed to be done, but the wards it seemed were closed. The curtain had finally come down. Sanglah was now off limits to anyone except staff and legitimate visitors. The message was very clear, "Thank you, but no thank you."

I headed towards the car park and would exit the hospital through the emergency section. I was pleased to see a familiar face as I approached the doors. Karen, my friend that had been tackling the medical records since day one was still trying to keep data bases up to date and was jotting down more notes at the E.R. admissions desk. She looked up as I approached and was equally pleased to see me.

"Hey Kim! Good to see you, I've got a message from David and Claire. They're trying to find you."

"Who?"

"David, Dr. David Marsh, you would have met him on the wards on Sunday."

"Hmmmm . . . Marsh?"

"Guy with a ponytail and glasses."

"Oh Dr. Ponytail! Why didn't you say so? Are they here?"

"Upstairs at a press conference, you know where the admin building is don't you? They're all up there."

"Thanks I'll go check it out."

I made my way up to the second floor and had a brief déjà vu as I remembered climbing the stairs on Sunday trying desperately to get permission for the volunteer Doctors to assist. The administrator's office was to the left but the press conference was at a room to the end of a corridor on my far right. The room was packed mostly with journalists that fired questions one after the other at the panel of hospital administrators in the front of the room. I could see David and Claire at the back of, and on the opposite side of the crowd. I pushed through as best I could, excusing myself as I went, dodging microphones and cameras to get to the good doctor and his wife on the other side. We greeted each other in a low whisper as one member of the press fired a controversial question at the panel.

"Sir, do you believe that moving the victims so soon was detrimental to the outcome, as we now know that some patients did die in transit?"

The medical director answered. "Yes, I do believe this could be so. Some of these patients were much too unstable to be moved. We could have looked after them just as well here. I do believe that the outcome would have been better if these patients had been left here for treatment."

David immediately lost his composure and started shouting at the top of his voice and all eyes were upon us.

"That's bullshit! That's absolute bullshit! You couldn't handle it! You just couldn't handle it!" David turned to address the audience. "If you journos want to know the real story, talk to me!! I'll tell you the real story!! This is crap!" He said as he gestured towards the panel that looked shocked by his outburst and immediately closed the meeting. Claire hustled David to the exit scolding him as she did.

"You shouldn't have done that dear! Look what a scene you've caused!"

"What d'ya mean? It's wrong. It's bloody wrong! There's no way they could have handled those cases here, you know that!"

"We all know that, they're just saving face, you know what it's like here, isn't that right Kim?"

"Yes, you're probably right. They wouldn't have had a chance here, and most of those that died in transit would not have had a chance anywhere, but you've got to try. You couldn't just leave them here."

As we left the crowd ahead of the journalists most of whom were still packing up their equipment or comparing notes, an Australian woman called out to us from behind.

"Excuse me, excuse me, would you mind if I just asked a few questions? Julie's my name, Julie Davies from The Age. You guys were obviously there and I wondered if I could have a quick word?"

David was obliging even though he was still fuming from the comments that had been made a few minutes earlier.

Julie wanted to talk more, but was in a hurry to keep up with the pack of journalists that were obviously en route to the next press conference. She gave us her card and we made arrangements to meet the following day at the Hard Rock Hotel for coffee and a chat although David was not sure that he would attend.

"Don't know that I'll join you, Sis. I've had it up to here with press! This lass seems like a nice enough girl, but I've just had enough. You know in I.C.U on Sunday some journo got decked by one of the other Doc's?"

"Really? Do tell! I wonder if it was the same guy that I nearly decked over in the E.R.?"

"Well this guy just walks into the I.C.U. and starts panning his camera across the poor blokes that are lying there starkers, some o' them as you know looked like they might not make it, so this Doc turns around and says "If you don't turn that camera off right now mate I'll deck ya." So this guy says something like, "You can't do that I've got rights!" and he carries on filming".

"And?"

"And so this Doc knocks him fair off his feet with a right hook and this guy looks at him and says "You just assaulted me! You punched me!" and the Doc says "Yeh I did, you want to see my round house kick as well?" So then the guy looks at me and says "Did you see that? That guy assaulted me and look my camera's bloody well ruined! Did you see that, you're a witness!" and I says "I didn't see a bloody thing mate I must have blinked and missed it!" . . . you should have seen his face it was priceless!"

"Haaa! I needed a laugh like that, best bloody laugh I've had this week!" I chuckled.

"Yep, I'd say so! They've got a nerve some of these journos! Well, . . . I think I'd like to go down to the Melati to check one of the Indonesian ladies that we worked on, see how she's doing. Want to join us Kim? Reckon we might need your language skills if we want to get the story straight down there."

"Sure, I'd be interested to see her myself, but I don't fancy your chances of getting in. I got knocked back this morning. Seems like they're starting to get cagey about foreigners snooping around."

"Oh well we'll give it a go ay Sis?"

At the Melati the story was the same. We were met by a wall of staff that were polite but firm in their message. They were obliging enough to let us peer through the windows, and David seemed to recognize the lady in question. At least she was still alive, although her chances were still slim. She had over fifty percent full thickness burns, and she would still have to battle the infection that would be reaching the peak of its initial assault on the third day.

The Melati ward itself was impressive, so much so that I had to check that we were in the right place! The staff wore gowns, gloves, masks and theatre boots. The floors were clean and the walls had been repainted. Air conditioners had been fitted, some of the old iron beds had been changed and all the linen looked fresh. A lot of work had been done since we had left the ward a battlefield on Sunday night.

David was allowed to check the lady's file, and was content that they were doing everything that could be done. We thanked the staff and bade them farewell, David and Clair shaking hands with each one in a gesture of sincere comradeship. As we walked towards the car park a voice called out from behind.

"Allo, allo, tunggu, allo, allo!" (Hello, hello wait!).

We turned to see an Indonesian man walking briskly towards us, waving his hand and signaling us to wait. He was slim and dark, obviously not from the wealthy sector and as he drew close he grasped David's arm with both hands and lowered his gaze to the floor.

"Termah kasih tuan . . . terimah kasih membantu isteri saya tuan!"

"Do I know this chap Kim? What's he saying?"

"He says thank you, he says you helped his wife and he says thank you."

"Yes! . . . Yes! . . . Now I remember this guy. Tell him it was my pleasure! Tell him we hope his wife will get well soon."

I relayed the message and by this time the man was gripping on to David's arm even tighter and as he trembled and sniffed his tears fell to the ground. Claire turned to walk away as she battled her emotions and David's eyes welled as he shook the man's arm. The distraught man thanked David yet again as he turned to walk back in to the ward.

Claire was standing a few feet away and was lucky to be wearing large tinted glasses that concealed her bulging eyes.

"Sorry about that." She said as she sniffed and dabbed her nose with her handkerchief. "It's just all coming back to me, it's all too much. It's so wrong all this! It's just all so wrong!"

David put his arm around Claire and comforted her as we walked. My phone rang and so I let the solemn couple stroll a few paces ahead while I took the call. It was my friend Shalimar. What would I tell her? I had still found no 'Robby's', 'Roberts' or 'Harpers'.

"Hi Shalimar, I wish I could tell you I had some news, but I don't I'm afraid."

"That's okay Kim. I just wanted to tell you something, something quite strange actually. Robby's mother called me and said that she has been to a psychic who says that Robby is in a two storey grayish colored building and that nobody knows he's there. Strange don't you think? Do you think it could be true? That he could be unconscious somewhere and no-one knows he's there?"

"What!? That's wrong to say that! That's bloody cruel! What if he isn't? What if he's dead? . . . It is possible that he's alive I suppose, but after three days? Unlikely! "

I stopped to think and once again this Mother's desperation tugged at my conscience. "I'll do some thinking, see if I can think of anywhere that fits that description Shali." I glanced over at the two storey emergency block that was indeed a grayish color, but he wasn't there, I had already checked several times.

"Let me work on it Shalimar, and I'll call you back."

David, Claire and I parted ways in the car park and I made for home where I would call every hospital that I could think of. There was a chance that Robby had been taken to some obscure facility and was amnesic or unconscious. I had to try, if it was my son I would search every inch of the Island, I would not rest until I had an answer, and I knew that Robby's mother would be feeling the same, but try as I might my efforts were in vain. I enlisted the help of Tony, the yellow pages and directory assistance, but all cards turned up blank. Robby was just not there.

13
Patrick is Failing
Wednesday October 16th

I had arranged to meet Chrissie at the lobby of the Hard Rock Hotel for breakfast. It would be good to see her again as we had not communicated since Sunday, and I was sure that we would have lots of catching-up to do.

Chrissie and I ordered coffee and sat at the restaurant that was usually bustling with tourists that would appease their appetites at the magnificent Hard Rock breakfast buffet which was nothing short of legendary. Today the appetites seemed to be meager or absent and the air was tense, the expressions on the faces of those that graced the brightly colored corridors were sinister, almost mask like.

The Hard Rock had become a conference center for the press as well as a briefing point for the families and friends of the victims. There was more grief walking in this Hotel than these walls should ever have seen. The brass busts of famous entertainers the likes of Elton John, Tina Turner and Chuck Berry stood as silent witness to those that paced the passageways in immeasurable sadness. Most would still be in a state of disbelief, a numbness that would beg mercy in a nightmare that was real.

Julie from the Melbourne Age would be here at 10 a.m., so Chrissie and I would have a few minutes to talk before she was due to arrive.

"How you doing Chrissie? Are you doing okay?" I enquired as the waitress delivered two cappuccinos.

"Fine, I'm okay . . . well most of time any way. It's just that well, sometimes I'll be sat at work doing something on the computer and I'll just lose it, I'll just start bawling for no reason!"

"You're back at work? Can't you get some time off? A couple of days to chill out and go away with John, take a break or something?"

"I could, that's not a problem, but I don't really want to, it's like if I'm busy I don't think about it but when there's nothing to do it all comes back to me again. I'd rather keep myself occupied, you know?"

"Yeah, Yeah I guess so. How's your patient? Patrick wasn't it?" I had struck a raw nerve and Chrissie took a deep breath as she looked into her coffee cup, stirring the white froth much more than she had needed to. Her answer was very brief as her face became heavy and drawn.

"Not so good."

"Oh." I decided not to prod any further but Chrissie continued to speak through deep stilted breaths and tears started to flow freely down her cheeks.

"He's in a coma, Patrick's in a coma. They said it's pretty dicey. I've kept in contact with his son, they're really nice people and he calls me to let me know how Pat's doing."

"Oh, I'm sorry Chrissie, I'm really sorry, but he was pretty badly burned you know. A lot that we sent out are not doing so good . . . It's the burns. It's bloody cruel!"

Many of the victims with severe burns had started to succumb to the massive infection from the combustion injury that had rendered the first line of defense of the immune system (the skin) useless. The massive assault of this injury would see the vital organs fail one by one. The kidneys, the heart, the liver and the brain would struggle desperately to maintain function and life. It was no wonder that fire, heat and burning were synonymous with the concept of what some believed to be 'hell'.

Chrissie cast her gaze out toward the ocean as she shared her thoughts. "I'm just worried that it could have been me, something I did, or didn't do that made him worse! . . . What if it was me?!"

"Chrissie! Don't even go there! You gave Patrick the best chance he had! How many other patients had their own nurse? He got the best care he could have had!"

"But I just can't believe it, you saw him, he was sitting there talking to me, told me all about his family and everything, just like he was going to be okay, and now this!?"

"Chrissie it's the burns! There's nothing more you could have done! It's just the way it is!"

"Yes, I suppose, but I still can't help thinking . . ."

"Then stop thinking, stop it! Promise me you won't have another thought about blaming yourself for this, promise me!?"

Chrissie drew in a deep sigh. "Yep . . . yep . . . okay . . . I'll try. Let's just hope he pulls out of this. I think I'm gonna go down there Kim, I've gotta go and see him again. I think I'll go to Adelaide before I go home to Perth."

"Good! Half your luck, I wish I could come with you!"

Julie the journalist looked hurried as she approached the table, files and notes in her hand; she was just ending a conversation on her phone as she pulled up a chair at our table.

"Sorry I'm a bit late girls. Deadlines . . . I tell you! Ahh, that coffee looks good! Can I get you girls a top up?"

Chrissie and I both declined as Julie fumbled through her wad of papers, looking for a blank note pad to write on.

"Thanks for coming here to do this today, you must be so busy with all this . . . now . . . if I can just get this pen to work!"

Julie was a pleasant woman with compassion and empathy, which was more than could be said for some members of the press that we had come across. Julie was a mother herself and was fully aware of the pain that people would be feeling. Her questions were delicate and relevant to the situations that Chrissie and I had encountered.

My phone was ringing incessantly and it seemed that wood and ice for the morgue were once again running in short supply. I would pass the calls on to those that I thought would be better able to assist with these commodities than myself and I wracked my brain to think of who might have these supplies; fish export agents, builders, party-ice company's etc.

The interview lasted for about an hour after which a photographer took our photographs. He instructed us to look 'pensive' as we gazed out to the ocean over the restaurants balcony . . . I wondered how else we were supposed to look? At least he hadn't asked us to watch the birdie and smile! We farewelled Julie who was on her way to yet another press conference and Chrissie informed me that a TV reporter had asked her for an interview and she wanted me to join her.

The television crew was setting up on the balcony that overlooked the swimming pool and as we walked towards them a young Australian man called out from behind us. I ignored him at first as I felt sure that I had no connection with anyone that might be staying here. We kept walking and he called out again as he quickened his pace to catch us.

"Hello! Hello! Excuse me . . . Hello!" I turned around and he looked directly at me although I could still not place this young man at all. "Hi . . . remember me?" He asked smiling.

"I'm sorry, I have to be honest, I've met so many people over the last few days . . ."

"Sure that's okay, but you'll remember my mate Stewy, you took him in the ambulance, he had a piece of glass in his neck."

"YES! . . . yes of course, now I remember! You're his mate that rode with us! How's Stewart? How's he doing?"

"Great! He's okay, and they got the glass out straight away when he got home, he's doing good now but they said it was really close."

"I bet! Look I can't stop for long now, but if you talk to Stewy tell him I said hello!"

The young man shook my hand firmly as he spoke. "Will do, I'll tell him that for sure."

Over on the Hard Rock Hotel balcony the female presenter stood with the television crew. She was an attractive young blonde woman in a bright red tailored suite with perfectly coifed hair and make-up. She busied herself silently rehearsing her lines as she looked down at her clipboard. She looked up briefly as Chrissie introduced us and little more was said as Chrissie excused herself to visit the bathroom leaving me to the mercy of the cameraman and the crew. This is where I learned my first lesson on television interviews . . . always find out what they are going to ask you before the cameras start rolling!

The film crew placed me in exactly the right background setting and the lights glared as the officious young reporter took up her position a few feet away to my right.

"Okay, everybody ready?" The cameraman enquired as the rest of the team signaled that everything was in order. "Okay . . . we're rolling."

"Sheree Dale here in Bali reporting for you on 'Live Tonight' and we're speaking with Kim Patra an Australian nurse who has been working with the victims in a Denpasar hospital since early Sunday morning. Kim can you tell us what you think about the latest reports that claim that the Australian Government had been forewarned of these attacks and that this information had been withheld from the general public?"

I had heard nothing of this and was caught completely off guard. "What?"

"What comment would you make if these accusations were indeed true?"

"I'm sorry this is the first I've heard of it!"

But the relentless reporter was not going to give up easily. She wanted a sensation and she was determined to get it!

"Well, what would you say for example to the parents and the loved ones of those that were killed if the Australian Government had indeed been aware that Bali was a target for terrorism?"

"What the hell would you say to them?" I replied as I started to walk away.

"Cut! . . . Cut! . . . Okay scrap that one. Where's the other nurse?"

Chrissie was just walking out of the bathroom as I headed back to the restaurant that would lead me to the lobby.

"That was quick!" Chrissie seemed surprised that I had finished the interview this quickly so I decided to forewarn her about the crew's intentions before she too was put on the spot.

"Yeh, you're damn right it was quick! Take my advice don't do it!"

"That bad huh?"

I put on my very best television voice as I mimicked the reporters stance. "Can you tell us what you think about the latest reports that claim that the Australian Government had been warned of terrorist attacks in Bali and that this information had been withheld from the general public?"

"What?!" Chrissie was as taken a back as I had been.

"Told you! Don't do it! Anyway I'd better go. Tony just called to say that the new mattresses that I ordered for Sanglah are ready for delivery so I have to be there to pay for them."

"Okay, let me know if you need a hand. I'll see you around, Kim. You take care."

"Yeh, you too . . . Hey Chrissie, say hello to Adelaide for me will you?"

"Will do!"

Chrissie and I parted ways, and I headed for the car park where the M.A.S.H. machine was waiting. The old jalopy obliged me a smooth ride back into the hospital and I stopped at a friend's office on the way to collect the money that was to be used to pay for the mattresses. During the brief visit Kevin and his wife Jan, another expatriate couple that had been organizing donations, informed me that an association would be formed to handle all the money that was pouring in. They told me that I had been nominated as a signatory for the bank account as I was an Indonesian citizen and would be able to sit on the committee of the organization; naturally I agreed.

Two large trucks carrying the mattresses were just pulling into the Sanglah car park as I searched for a vacant parking spot. I was surprised at the speed at which this bedding had been dispatched as I had only just ordered it this morning. I paid the driver of the trucks and a team of university students started to unload the ninety mattresses and seventy pillows. It wasn't until I started to approach the huge military storage tents that had been erected on the hospital lawns that I realized that something was not quite right. The mattresses were all double bed size, and not the single bed size that I had ordered!

The driver of the truck apologized profusely for the sizing error and promised to return before two o'clock with the correct sized mattresses. It was twelve thirty now so I would have time for lunch at the volunteer's canteen that was still in operation at the back of the emergency room block.

The same faces still worked tirelessly at feeding the masses and were no less cheerful for all their efforts. Everyone was served with a smile and the array of food was still as wonderful as it had been on Sunday. I chose a chicken sandwich and an orange juice and sat alone at one of the smaller tables. Shortly after settling myself down, I looked up and was delighted to see an old friend and colleague walking down the open corridors towards me. Dr Darma had a smile that stretched from one ear to the other. I stood up as she drew nearer and she greeted me warmly with a sincere embrace.

Darma was slimmer now than she once had been and there was an air of serenity about her that seemed to have developed after her recent brush with Dengue fever that had almost taken her life. She had a new found faith in her own spirituality, which was a common occurance when a Balinese had been severely ill or had narrowly escaped death.

"So Doc, it's great to see you! I heard you've been pretty busy, I saw a story on you in the morning paper!"

"Aww Ibu Kim! We all busy! I know you busy too! You come here on Sunday I know, I see you but no time to talk!"

"Oh that's for sure . . . we hardly had time to breathe! Now tell me about the man that you helped? I read about it in the paper!"

Darma did not completely lose her smile, I don't think I had ever seen her not smiling, but the corners of her mouth definitely softened as she looked down at the orange juice that had just been delivered for her at the table.

"Yes Ibu. It was terrible for this man. His legs gone . . . you know I just hold him as much I can. I just hold him and I try to stop the bleeding from his legs before he have to going to operation room . . . but he die, I can't help him he just die. He tell me . . . he tell me."

Darma's large brown doe eyes were filling with water but she still did not loose her smile.

"He say to me 'Tell my Mum I love her' before he go, but I never know his name!" she drew in a deep sigh, "maybe his Mum already know? I hope so."

"I'm sure she does Darma, I'm sure she does."

There was brief silence as we took some liquid refreshment, but my sandwich had somehow lost its appeal.

I made my way back to the large marquees that were receiving supplies and gave the inventory clerk notice of the seventy pillows as well as ninety mattresses that were due to arrive at any minute. All goods that had been received were being data based by the university students, and once my lot had been recorded I requested for a team to help me deliver the bedding to the wards where I would change those that were blood soaked and stained with the new ones, but my offer was flatly declined.

"No need Ibu," said the young man who had written down the details of the delivery. "We can handle it from here. You just leave what you bring here then we can do for distribution."

I was determined to finish the job that I had started and so I challenged the young man who had refused my assistance. "No you don't understand! I'm not a tourist, I live here I'm a nurse, I worked here all day on Sunday and I know where these mattresses are needed."

"Thank you Ibu, but we handle now. We fix for all don't you worry."

I could see that I was getting nowhere fast with this conversation and the trucks with the new mattresses had arrived, so I moved away from the tents to settle payment with the driver who informed me that I would get an extra thirty mattresses as the price on the smaller ones was cheaper. This was definitely a bonus, but I would still have liked to have had a hand in delivering them to the wards!

Turning back to face the tents, I saw teams of youths who were already moving the pillows using a convoy of supermarket trolleys and I thought better of interfering any further.

Earlier in the day I had received a message that some medicines had been received and were being held at Dr David 'Ponytail's' villa. There were still enough hours in the day and I could detour to Seminyak just north of Kuta to collect them, before I returned to my home.

I felt mildly embarrassed as Claire answered the door of the stylish villa. She was wrapped in a brightly colored beach sarong and appeared to have just woken from an afternoon nap.

"Oh sorry Claire! I've woken you up! I just came to pick up the medicines. I won't stay, go back to bed and finish your siesta."

"Not at all, don't be silly! Come on in David will be out in just a tick."

David emerged from the bedroom looking just as sleepy and sporting a floral sarong that matched Claire's. He seemed to be walking with his legs slightly bowed and he moaned as he stretched. This made me feel even worse at having disturbed this couple's afternoon slumber!

"Hello there Sis! Good to see you again, I've got pressies for you! A couple of bags of things I think you might be able to use over the next few weeks. Oooh!" David rubbed the small of his back as he lowered himself on to the sofa. "I swear every muscle in my body still aches after last Sunday! I tell you what, we should have worn a pedometer (step meter) on that day . . . how many miles do you think we did Sis?"

"Oh, lots!"

"I'd say", David agreed, "and I'm not as young as I thought I was either at least that's what my wife tells me any way."

"Oh I do not!" Claire retorted. "You're just as much of a stud as you always were you old fool!"

"Well I must be doing some thing right then!" David replied with a short burst of laughter as he gestured for the maid to come from the kitchen. "Be a darling and fetch those bags from the bedroom will you sweetie? My backs killing me other wise I'd get them myself."

"It seems to me that you could get used to having all these women around you waiting on you hand and foot!" I said in jest.

"What! They'd drive me mad; I'd have to share myself around too much!"

"Oh don't push your luck Dahante!" Claire replied raising her eyebrows as she scoffed at her husband's tomfoolery.

What a couple these two were, a perfect match, an exact fit. I wondered how often couples like this found each other and what it was that kept them in such a bond.

I kept my visit brief as I had promised, and loaded the medicines into the car. I bade farewell to the doctor and his wife and we promised to meet again at a candlelight gathering on the beach that had been scheduled for Sunday.

The shadows were long now as the evening drew near. The air was already laced with the scent of the incense as the dusk offerings of flowers and spices were laid out along the sides of the roads. My car was behaving remarkably well, as not only did she start on the first turn of the ignition, but the air conditioner and the cassette deck were working as well! My Sarah Mc Laughlin tape was playing and I had never really listened to her ballad with such intent as I did on this thirty minute drive to my Sanur home. 'In the Arms of the Angels' could have been written for us, for this island and all that we had seen over the past four days. Her voice was haunting and goose-bumps prickled the hairs on my neck as I listened over and over again to the same song.

"In the arms of the angels, fly away from here . . . From this dark cold hotel room, and the endlessness that you fear . . . You are pulled from the wreckage of your silent reverie . . . You're in the arms of the angels . . . May you find some comfort there." (Sarah McLaughlin)

14
Give Us Our Dead
Thursday October 17th

I would have been wiser to stay at home on this morning, as the day proved to be a frustrating succession of events that would have me chasing my tail and achieving very little at all. Today was the day of Banks and I had been summoned along with the three other signatories to sign for accounts that would receive the donations pouring in from all over the globe. We would be driven to the brink of insanity over the shortcomings of the bank staff that had us sign incorrect papers no less than five times!

The organization that we had formed was to be called Yayasan Kemanusian Ibu Pertiwi (The Association for Humanitarian Aid of Mother Pertiwi . . . The Goddess of life) and was abbreviated to 'Y.K.I.P.'. The association would initially concentrate its efforts on improving the local medical facilities and would later expand in collaboration with another new foundation - YKIDS, to include an educational support program for the children who had been orphaned or whose families had suffered financial hardship as a result of the bomb. This small band of founders quickly grew to a board of members, committees, and subcommittees. The men and women at the helm of this charter were true professionals, heads of corporations and skilled business persons, and I had no desire to try and match the likes of these leaders. I would nominate myself for the bottom of the 'Medical Preparedness' sub committee. There was only one thing I wanted from all of this and that was my kits. Trauma disaster kits that I could distribute if this should ever happen again. I wanted to be ready; I wanted to have what they would need next time, the Vijay's, David's, John's and Priya's that would walk out of nowhere ready to give their time and their skills. I would have the scalpels and gloves, the I.V. lines and fluids, the dressings and the bandages, all the things that would be needed for the initial treatment of the victims that were as yet unknown. This was my vision.

I sat daydreaming in the opulent foyer of the bank, waiting for yet another set of papers to sign and the sound of my telephone broke my daze. Shalima was calling and she would certainly be able to help me pass the time in conversation while I sat waiting for the bank papers to be typed up yet again.

"Hi Kim, How are you holding up?"

"Fine! Believe it or not I'm bored! I'm stuck sitting around this bank here waiting to sign accounts for the foundation. How's yourself? Is there any news on your nephew Robby?"

"Well kind of, His Mother went to a psychic and . . ." I interrupted assuming that she was about to repeat the story that I had heard a few days ago.

"No, wait, listen to this. His mother went to another spirit medium and got the same story! He's in a two story building and no-one knows that he's there!"

The hairs on the back of my neck stood on end as I battled to digest what I had just heard. "WHAT?! How can it be? It's been almost five days Shalima! How can he still be alive if he's alone and no-one knows he's there?"

"I don't know Kim, I just don't know! It's all too weird, but you can't help believing that there must be something to it if two separate readings have come up with the same information!"

I could not believe that Robby was still alive and so I offered another theory for this strange occurrence. "Perhaps he is there Shalima! Perhaps he is . . . but not in any shape or form that we can see! You and I have been here too long Shalima you know what it's like here. The spirits walk, maybe that's what these mediums are seeing. It's not Robby in his physical form, it's his shadow, his spirit still walking."

By the time I returned to Sanur the day was almost gone and I could not help but thinking what a waste of a day this had been. There would only just be enough time to shower and change before I had to leave my home and children once again. The Australian Consulate was to hold a meeting at the Radisson Hotel at 6 p.m. to address the relatives of the victims and the expatriate community at large. The Australian Ambassador would attend as well other Government officials from Australia & Jakarta.

The air was tense in the private lobby that was situated in the west wing of the hotel. The congregation of about two hundred people would be addressed in the luxurious ballroom that had been used to accommodating much grander and far more cheerful occasions than this. Security was tight, and members of the press were strictly off limits. The general feeling among the crowd that milled around the lobby was still one of shock and disbelief. Many looked tired; exhausted from days of toiling continuously as part of an army of volunteers that were still waging a tireless battle in the aftermath of an attack that could only be termed as a senseless slaughter. Others looked drawn and empty. These were the ones that had been bereaved, torn from the ones they loved by warmongers and cowardly jackals, by evil shadows that could not be seen or attacked in counter. There was nowhere for the grieving mob to direct it's anger or lay blame, no one they could target as the perpetrator, nothing to which they could give substance and direction for the hatred and bitterness that brewed.

Many could not make sense of the way that their dead had been interned in a slaughterhouse prison, just another case file number in a stack of many others. When would they be given what was rightly theirs to hold? When would they be allowed to take their own flesh and blood to their homeland where the rites of passage could be performed and the dead finally laid to rest?

We were ushered into the ballroom where rows of chairs had been assembled. A small group of larger more elaborate chairs had been positioned in a row facing the audience and a podium was situated to the left of the panel. The congregation was seated and it was a capacity crowd with all seats taken and a further fifty or so still standing at the rear of the hall, including myself. I could not help thinking that Ross Tysoe, the Australian Consul General (Bali office), looked as if the huge gold lame and velvet chair would swallow him up! He looked small, deflated, pale and drained of his usual zest; he sat quietly and motionless as he gazed at the floor. David Chaplin, Ross's assistant did not attend and I assumed that he was resting after the mammoth task that he and his staff had tackled over the past five days.

The officials addressed the crowd as diplomatically and delicately as they could. The audience would be given the opportunity to address the panel at the end of the briefing, and it had already become apparent that the congregation was divided, literally, into two groups. Those seated to the right of the center aisle were expatriates and those that were seated to the left were the families of the victims. Both of these groups had very different and conflicting issues that needed to be addressed; for the families it was the loss of life and for the expatriates it was the loss of livelihood.

The microphone was passed around to those that had raised their hands, and the first man to speak launched an emotional plea to the government representatives that echoed the emotions of so many.

"Mr. Ambassador, I would just like to know the logic behind why my niece, whom I have positively identified three days ago, is still in the morgue and why they won't let me take her out?!"

The tall austere Ambassador took the podium and tried to answer the man as best he could.

"Thank you Sir, and firstly I would like to extend all our sympathy to you and your family. This is such a tragic and trying time for all of you, and indeed for all of us. I believe there are certain forensic procedures that have to be completed before any more bodies will be released so as to make absolutely sure that there is no confusion in the matter."

"I'm sorry Mr. Ambassador, but there IS NO confusion in this matter. I can understand how other bodies may take time to identify, but the girl that I have seen is DEFINATELY my niece! Where's the bloody compassion here! I have come here for one reason and one reason only, to take our Angie home and I can't bloody well do it! We want answers not sympathy!"

There was a general hum of support from the audience who nodded in agreement with this man's plea.

The Ambassador was at a loss for words and promised that he would do 'whatever he could' to assist this man and others that may be in a similar situation.

The line of questioning from the group to my right was very different and addressed the matter of travel bans to Indonesia, and in particularly Bali. The economy here was almost exclusively reliant on tourism, and if the bans remained in place the economy would surely flounder forcing many businesses into bankruptcy and their redundant employees into poverty. While the financial predictions of the residents were a valid concern, the blood of several hundred victims and the wounds inflicted on this island were still too fresh to ignore. The perpetrators of this deed had not yet been caught and we were still at considerable risk for further attacks. One of the men on the relative's side shouted his concerns across the room.

"You wouldn't be so bloody quick to worry about your pockets if it was your kids that had been blown away mate! I say the bans are too late if anything and now they should bloody well stay!"

The audience broke into a general hum as each agreed or disagreed with the outburst. The air was tense and what was about to happen would test the constitution of everyone in the room.

A power blackout plunged us into total darkness. There was instant silence as we waited for the ground to shake or the walls to crumble. What had caused this? Was it something close-by, or an explosion at a distant location that had caused the electricity to fail? There were people in this room that had been very close to the Sari Club when the bomb had exploded. Their senses must be reeling, reliving the few brief moments of darkness as the power failed and the lights went out before the second of the two explosions engulfed the busy nightclub.

This crowded hotel ballroom was suspended in fearful anticipation for less than a minute and yet it seemed to go on forever. I half expected hysteria to break out in the audience, but the silence continued each one straining their senses to detect the cause of this blackness. As the lights came on the room filled with a general din of chatter, and silent prayers of relief were uttered by many, myself included.

15
Candles in the Wind
Sunday, 20th October

A full week had passed since that fateful day at Sanglah hospital, which had most certainly changed us all in one way or another. This afternoon we would meet again; Dr David (Ponytail), Claire, Karen (medical data-base volunteer) and myself. We were to convene at the lobby of the Hard Rock Hotel at three o'clock for an appearance on the Australian Telethon Appeal, after which we would attend a candlelight vigil on the sands of Kuta beach in honor of those who had been taken.

The hotel lobby, which opened directly onto the Center Stage bar and entertainment area, had all but lost its party atmosphere. It was not more than two weeks ago that Tony and I had watched Jimmy Barnes belt out his nostalgic repertoire to a packed audience; now the posters promoting music and decadent buffets had been replaced by hand-written sheets of paper directing the journalists and bereaved families to press conferences and Consular briefings. This grand hotel had gone from merry-makers playground to mausoleum in a fitting transformation for the guests that she now housed.

As we gathered in the lobby several other friends arrived to join us in the wake-like atmosphere of the front bar; among them were Melina, Katrina and her daughter Brianna, Melody, Marius and Matt. We recounted the events of the past week, compared notes on our experiences and how each of us was coping. I was shocked and saddened to hear of another young expatriate woman with whom I was acquainted, that had lost her husband.

Karen told us the story. "I think Jane's having trouble accepting it," she said with compassion. "Poor kid, she's so young."

Melina was equally sympathetic. "Who wouldn't have trouble

accepting it? One minute your husband is there with you and the next minute he's gone!"

"Well this is even harder," Karen went on. "They haven't found him yet, and listen to this . . . he came to the house on the Sunday after the bomb and spoke to the maid, he told her to take care of his wife and child!"

"What!?"

". . . and then on the Sunday night Jane had reached over to comfort her three year old son in his bed, and the space where John usually slept was hot! It makes you wonder doesn't it? I think that she's only just come to terms with the fact that he's really gone. One of her friends took her to a 'Balian' (spirit medium) and John spoke to her, he told her that his head and shoulders were at the morgue, but that his lower half was still at the bomb site . . . so go figure? It's all too weird!"

Seeking the guidance of spirit mediums after the death of a loved one is a standard practice among the Balinese. The words of the deceased channeled through a 'Balian' are considered as good as will and testimony and the séance was often used to settle unfinished business. I had once witnessed such a séance where the spirit communicated his concerns regarding such trivial matters as owing the local warung (store) a few hundred rupiah for a box of matches. The spirit medium's information had been correct to the finest detail.

While the majority of Indonesians are Islam with smaller pockets of Christianity dotted throughout the archipelago most still hold similar spiritual and metaphysical beliefs. Jane's husband, John, was in fact a Christian from Sumatra.

"Well let's hope she's okay through all of this. Was she a patient of yours, Kim?"

"No why?"

"She's pregnant, about three months I think."

I cursed out loud. There were no words to describe these thieves of justice who had slaughtered fathers, mothers, sons and daughters. Even animals of the lowest order had more compassion than this.

Dr. David ambled up to our table and broke the temporary lull in conversation with what I first thought was a joke!

"Hey, d'ya hear about the girl that walked away from the Sari Club unscathed, then went with her injured friend down to Darwin . . . and got eaten by a bloody crocodile!?"

"Oh sick David! Who thought that one up?!" I retorted.

"What d'ya mean? It's bloody well true!" David replied as another member of our party confirmed that the bizarre story was indeed authentic.

"Well . . . I guess that goes to show that when your number's up, your number is really up!" I philosophized, lost for any other words to describe this poor young girl's fate.

Another 'believe it or not story' was told as we finished our drinks and readied ourselves for the afternoon's shoot.

"Well there's a few people around here that need to be thrown to the crocodiles if you ask me. Did you hear about the local woman who sold Aqua (bottled drinking water) for fifty thousand rup's (AUD$10.00) a bottle on the night of the bomb?!"

"What!? Is that true?!" I could hardly believe that someone could be so opportunistic.

"Apparently so . . . I bet she'll have a few 'karma' worries after pulling a little stunt like that!"

Our telethon appearance on the rooftop of the hotel was brief as we stood just below the famous four; Paul, George, John & Ringo cast in bronze stood immortal against the Kuta sky-line. We each had the opportunity to say a brief word to 'Australia' and Karen surprised us all by saying hello to her Mum on camera!

The sky was turning brilliant hues of orange as the late afternoon sun flaunted its magnificent parade of color and was undaunted by the grief that immersed us. Our small group had grown considerably with the addition of those who had come to gather in mourning. The conversation had become scant and there was an air of introspection as we made our way down to the Kuta shoreline. Kneeling in the sand we prepared ourselves in anticipation of the darkness that drew near. Struggling to light our candles we sheltered each flame from the persistent sea breeze as a frail voice from behind me started to warble the first few lines of 'Amazing Grace.'

By the end of the first verse the throng was belting it out, giving this age-old hymn all the emotion that it demanded. There was a brief silence after the song as each of us offered our own silent prayers for the dead. The crowd stood and there was a general din of chatter as words of sympathy and courage were exchanged.

Dr. Marsh and I embraced briefly and he offered some solace as we did so. "You did great kiddo, you did just great. We did our best and we couldn't have done more than that Sis, you know that." These words confirmed that he had been feeling exactly the same way as I had. We had relived every minute of Sunday the 13th, and had meticulously dissected all that we had done searching for fault or reason that we should have, or could have been able to do more.

As the crowd milled around saying their last goodbyes, a man approached me and politely requested a brief word for a radio talk show in Sydney. He dialed the Australian studio from a large Nokia hand set and asked me to answer his questions by speaking into the telephone.

"So tell me Kim, I hear that you have spent quite a lot of time at the Denpasar hospital assisting with evacuations is that correct?"

"Yes, . . . Yes that's right."

"Now we are all aware that initially the Indonesian Government did not allow it's nationals to be airlifted to Australia, but now the ban has been lifted for several days and it seems that a lot of the injured Balinese do not want to go? Can you tell us why you think this is so? It seems to me that if you had the chance to be treated overseas that you would jump at the opportunity? Is there perhaps an anti-Australian feeling here do you think?"

"No! Oh no not at all . . . quite the opposite in fact! You see there is something here that Westerners might find hard to comprehend. The whole concept of life and death here is so completely different to our way of thinking. A Balinese would rather die on his own soil than struggle for life in a foreign land. If he or she died here in Bali, their spirit would know the way; if they died in an unfamiliar place their soul might be lost. A Balinese would value spiritual and cultural beliefs over the medical outcome of his condition, even if his own life were at stake."

"That's very interesting indeed. Have you personally encountered any aggression as a foreigner over this past week?"

"No, not at all."

"Thank you very much Kim Patra. This has been Ian Wells reporting to you live from Kuta beach . . . Bali."

I felt a wave of exhaustion flow over me as I watched the remainder of the crowd disperse. Dr. Marsh and his wife Claire would leave for Melbourne on tonight's flight, and we exchanged contact numbers before we said our final farewells. The couple looked more than weary as they made their way along the sand, and I felt much the same way.

In eight days I had not stopped working; breaking only to perform the mandatory tasks of eating, sleeping and attending to personal hygiene. Tomorrow I would rest. I would stay in my home, take a long bath and try very, very hard to do nothing at all.

Monday, 21st October

It was hardly daylight and my telephone was already ringing. Susannah was in her ninth month of pregnancy and I could not ignore the call.

"Kim, I am sorry to disturb you, I think my waters have broken."

My patient had started contractions two weeks before her due date, and I was bound to accompany her through her long twenty-one hour labor.

At four fifteen the following morning Purnami (child of the full moon) was born and as I handed this little beauty to her Mother I thought of all that I had witnessed over these past ten days, all the life that had been lost, and how this child was a poignant reminder that life continued on regardless.

As this proud Mother nursed her infant for the first time she spoke.

"Do you think you'll stay Kim? Will you stay here after all that's happened?"

I pondered the question briefly as I took stock of all that had transpired and how our lives had changed.

"Yes . . . yes I'll stay."

This island was scarred, her wounds still deep and fresh and her people still in mourning. Bali as we had known her had changed, there was fear and uncertainty, but for all this, for all that she was, or was not, Bali was still my home.

Epilogue

I have recollected and recorded the events in this book as accurately as possible, however I am only human, and to recall a part of your life in which you have witnessed events and circumstances one could only term as inhumane, has not been an easy task. Writing these memoirs has been a healing exercise for me, and I have resurrected memories that I have needed to share with so many others, whose minds and lives have been tainted with the tragedy that was "The Bali Bomb'.

In the initial weeks following the attack, many volunteers including myself searched websites and tabloids, looking for the names of those that we had treated, concerned at how they had fared. Sadly we saw the names of so many that we recognized who had succumbed to their injuries days or weeks following the attack. All of the patients that I had listed from the Sanglah intensive care units, excepting 'Aden' and 'Saiful' were fated to pass on. The girls that Vijay and Priya had worked so hard to stabilize in the Melati ward's side room, would also fail one by one.

The Canadian man at the Wangaya Hospital with the head injury and affected speech, did not survive, slipping into a coma shortly after he arrived in Australia. The 'Big American' for whom I had held grave fears did survive, and was treated in Singapore where he was released to return to the United States in time for Christmas. The Australian amputee that was evacuated from the same hospital survived, as did Stewart, the man with the shrapnel wound to his neck.

Chrissie's patient eventually came out of his coma, and is still battling the long road to recovery. Chrissie visited 'Patrick' in Adelaide and then again in Perth, and the two have formed a very special bond.

Dr. Art Sorrell never found the man for whom he was concerned, and we are forced to assume that he, along with countless others, did not survive.

'Robby' was never found. His family was presented with a box of 'D.N.A. positive' human remains, along with so many other families, who were given similar packages or nothing at all. For these families grieving would be a cruel path of nothingness; nothing to hold, nothing to see and nothing to release. The acknowledgment of death would become an insurmountable hurdle, with their only comfort being that they were by no means alone in their grief.

The Denpasar hospitals, including Sanglah, Wangaya, R.S.A.D., Kasih Ibu, Prima Medika and Graha Asih have received more than their fair share of criticism for the way this disaster was handled. Regardless of all that has been said, when one takes into consideration the lack of available equipment and skilled personnel, and the magnitude of the situation, the task that was performed was admirable. The teams that worked in these facilities saved countless of lives; Sanglah hospital alone admitting almost three hundred casualties and performing countless operations in a matter of hours. You cannot help but salute the efforts of these men and women.

The 'Travelling Doctors' that had paced the wards on that fateful Sunday, returned to their respective countries. Most were honored by their profession and their countrymen for the service that they had given. Dr. David and Claire Marsh were given a civil reception in their home town of Melbourne, and were later awarded as 'Victorians of the Year'.

The massive body of workers and volunteers that remained on the island, would once again group, to attend events that would range from spiritual Balinese cleansing ceremonies to a massive peace concert.

Counseling services were offered to all volunteers at various posts around the island. A medical screening program was implemented for those that had worked in the morgue, many of whom had started to exhibit signs and symptoms of disease that may have been contracted in the less than hygienic conditions in which they worked. The morgue remained a hive of activity, with volunteers and forensics experts battling to identify the last of the human remains. The final remnants would not be released until six months after the bombing.

Many of those that worked closely with the dead have reported strange occurrences, sightings or sensation of touch from another realm. Ghostly faces were seen at the morgue; a shadow of a man drinking beer was seen by several witnesses at ground zero; a Balinese woman in trance at a temple ceremony spoke with the voice of an Australian girl, and actually asked for a drink of Fanta. (The woman had no prior knowledge of the English language). The lights on burned-out cars were reported to flash and a flimsy temple umbrella inside Paddy's Pub remained completely intact, despite the fact that cars and shop fronts, for almost a fifty meter radius, were completely burned out.

The stories of these spiritual encounters are many, but from all the reports that I have heard, there seems to be one common factor that deserves comment, and this is that none of those that bore witness to these accounts felt threatened.

Massive fundraising efforts were launched, not only locally, but worldwide, and the many organizations that had taken up the cause in Bali came together to form 'The Bali Recovery Group'. This conglomerate of associations tackled the massive task and the logistical nightmare of locating the victims and their families, and of passing judgment on who should receive assistance and who should not.

Since the events of October 2002, life as we had once known it on this island has changed. Gone are the Robinson Crusoe days of a 'kira-kira' (near enough is good enough) existence; life has now become a more exact science with personal security one of the foremost concerns. Bomb threats at International Schools and Hotels have become commonplace, and security check points that had once been unheard of are now a standard procedure. Each and every one of us has become acutely aware of the strangers or vehicles near by; we lock our cars and homes, and monitor the whereabouts of our children more closely than ever before.

Global terrorism is now a reality from which no country can claim immunity. The perpetrators are shadows without shape or form. They can infiltrate any community anywhere and at any time.

Bali is no longer a jewel apart; no longer the safe haven we once thought it was, exempt from the conflict and terror that laps at her shores. Through all that this island has suffered, the spirit of the community, both expatriates and Balinese, remains undaunted, her beauty and character still remains supreme.

The Tribute

Many awards have been issued in recognition of those who gave service in the hours, days, weeks and months that followed the Bali Bomb. Many of these have been based on nationality, profession or magnitude of deed.

Hundreds of volunteers, professionals, groups and organizations gave above and beyond the call of duty in a collective force that rose to the colossal challenge that had to be met during the aftermath of the bomb. It is my intention to mention as many of those individuals and associations as possible on a list that is published on our website as a tribute to them all (http//:www.inthearmsoftheangels-bali.com).

I make no pretense to claim that this list is either accurate or complete, for indeed it never could be. Many names will not appear on this list and I make prior apologies for those that have been missed either through lack of information or the time constraints that have been put upon me.

There is one group that does not appear on this list and yet I feel they deserve to be mentioned here. These people are the victims of the bomb itself; the patients that filled the wards and corridors in those first horrific hours after fire and force inflicted wounds that could only be termed as cruel. I have heard the comment, more than several times, that the bravery and calm exhibited by those injured was remarkable. The protests and screams that one might expect from such a wounded throng were just not there. An example of this phenomenon might best be recounted by the story of a young man who had been badly burned on his face and chest. He had been offered pain relief, and sensing that this medication was in short supply he instructed the medic to "give it to someone that needs it more than me." The man died shortly after this outstanding act of selflessness.

So many stories like this will never be told and many accounts of heroism will have been lost with the lives of those that we tried to save.

For all of those who toiled, please accept this as your personal tribute.